MARKETING

Tom Arhontoudis

George Brown College

Pearson Canada Inc., 26 Prince Andrew Place, North York, Ontario M3C 2H4.

9780134771229

1 18

Library and Archives Canada Cataloguing in Publication

Arhontoudis, Tom, author
    Marketing / Tom Arhontoudis (George Brown College).

ISBN 978-0-13-477122-9 (spiral bound)

    1. Marketing—Textbooks. 2. Textbooks. I. Title.

HF5415.A74 2018   658.8   C2017-906425-8

Contents

Pearson FlexText

Essential Employability Skills

Top skills employers seek:

Success in any sector is dependent upon more than core academic knowledge or technical and occupational skills. Employers need critical thinkers, problem solvers, and leaders to tackle the challenges of today's workplace. Employees with successful career paths learn to communicate effectively, engage appropriately with others, and be self-reliant. Effective career readiness and employability strategies develop the whole learner and incorporate personal and social capabilities; critical thinking and problem-solving skills; and academic and occupational knowledge.

That is what Pearson FlexText is all about.

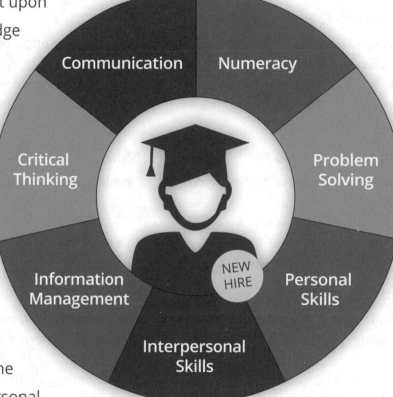

For more information on Pearson's commitment to employability, visit **pearsoned.com/employability**.

Pearson FlexText helps bridge the skills gap and helps students and instructors make the most of valuable face-to-face class time.

We created this resource to help students achieve academic success while also developing the key skills that hiring managers value in candidates.

Communication Skills

Defining skill areas: reading, writing, speaking, listening, presenting, and visual literacy

Students may not be developing their reading skills because they do not have access to course materials – either by choice or by circumstance. FlexTexts are affordable and accessible. FlexTexts include learning objectives and chapter summaries in combination with concise discussions of key topics to support reading comprehension, and provide individual and group activities that afford students the opportunity to practice their writing and communication skills.

Numeracy Skills

Defining skill areas: understanding and applying mathematical concepts and reasoning, analyzing and using mathematical data, and conceptualizing

This FlexText is designed to be an in-class activity workbook, one that allows faculty to provide instructional support to students as they apply mathematical and statistical analysis across a range of activities.

Critical Thinking & Problem-Solving Skills

Defining skill areas: analyzing, synthesizing, evaluating, decision making, creativity, and innovative thinking

The exercises and activities found in this FlexText are not simply factual, recall, or "skill and drill" activities. They engage students at different levels of Bloom's Taxonomy to help students develop critical thinking and problem-solving skills.

Information Management Skills

Defining skill areas: gathering and managing information, selecting and using appropriate tools and technology for a task or project, computer literacy, and internet skills

Not all of the exercises in a FlexText are pen-and-paper activities. Many require students to engage with online information and assets to help them investigate how to analyze and solve an array of problems and challenges.

Interpersonal Skills

Defining skill areas: teamwork, relationship management, conflict resolution, leadership, and networking

FlexText is designed to be brought into class. It can help to facilitate group work and collaborative problem solving, and activities can be implemented in ways that help students to develop their interpersonal skills.

Personal Skills

Defining skill areas: managing self, managing change, being flexible and adaptable, engaging in reflexive practice, and demonstrating personal responsibility

Making the decision to purchase course materials and actively engage with course content is one of the first steps toward demonstrating personal responsibility for success in school. The page layout of a FlexText also encourages note taking and promotes the development of strong study skills.

1

What Is Marketing?

LEARNING OBJECTIVES

 LO1 Define marketing and understand the definition of marketing

LO2 Outline the steps of the marketing process

LO3 Identify and define the 4Ps that make up the marketing mix

LO4 Explain the relationship of exchange and why it is required in marketing

LEARN...

Whether you realize it or not, marketing is everywhere and without even reading up on this discipline, most of us already know quite a lot about it. Marketing affects most of the day-to-day experiences that we as consumers have, and it is an essential part of any business operation.

We know and experience marketing every day. It's in our experience of our favourite products, the price that we pay for those products, the ads that we see and hear for them, and the promotional products we sample at our favourite supermarket. Marketing also educates us on the price that consumers want to pay for a product or service and the channel and format that they want to be communicated to.

In this introductory chapter on marketing, you'll learn what marketing is, the process marketers use to create valuable relationships with their customers, and the points of contact or *marketing mix* that are leveraged to build those valuable relationships. You'll also see how exchange—a *mutual interaction between two parties*—is vital to marketing's success.

What Is Marketing?

LO1 Define marketing and understand the definition of marketing

What is marketing and how would you explain this business concept, if you were asked?

The first few words that usually pop into a person's head are "advertising or sales". Others may define marketing as a mash-up of activities, such as public relations, sales promotion, advertising, social media, pricing, and distribution. But marketing is NOT just a television commercial, a pop-up ad, or a sales rep showing up at your front door trying to make a sale.

Today marketing is also about satisfying customer needs. If a marketer reaches out, engages consumers, and provides them with the proper product at the right price, through the right distribution and promotion channels, then the sale is easy. In fact, the customer might repeat the purchase, stay loyal to the brand, or even refer the product or service to friends and family. It is this sense of satisfying customer needs that differentiates today's marketing from marketing of the past. Business management guru Peter Drucker states that:

> The aim of marketing is to make selling unnecessary ... the aim of marketing is to understand your customer so well the product or service fits him and sells itself. (Drucker, 2012)

Official Definition of Marketing

There is no universally accepted definition of marketing, and, as a student of marketing, it is important to appreciate that the term "marketing" means different things to different people.

Marketing is more than just a sale; it's a "value-laden" exchange between an organization and consumers. According to the American Marketing Association:

> Marketing is the activity, set of institutions, and processes for creating, communicating, delivering, and exchanging offerings that have value for customers, clients, partners and society at large. (American Marketing Association)

Beyond the sale, the cumulative function of marketing is to communicate and deliver value to, and create value for, the customer. The most successful companies engage in very consumer-oriented marketing, and companies spend enormous amounts of time, money, and resources examining the everyday lives of their customers to create products that fill a need. Examples of companies that are known for creative, leading-edge marketing are Disney, Apple, and Coke.

You've probably had a Coke or two in your lifetime.

What was it that lured you to the beverage in the first place? Was it the price? The promotion? The packaging? Or the product itself? And what caused you to have it again or not?

The Coca-Cola brand has been described by many as a marketing machine that has managed to constantly innovate and evolve its brand to keep pace with its consumers. Many would even say that this model marketer would not be the global giant that it is, if it wasn't for its marketing acumen and prowess. The red and white logo is recognized by almost 94% of the world's population and this has allowed them to expand its product offering beyond cola beverages to bottled water, juices, orangeades, isotonics, teas, energy drinks, milk, coffee, and even beer.

Over the years, companies like Coke have dramatically increased their marketing budgets in hope that they could establish brands that deliver products and services that customers love and keep coming back for. Coke has remained relevant to marketers for 125 years by staying topical and following what their customers value, love, and appreciate.

Practice...

1. What is the definition of marketing?
   a. Marketing is the advertising of a product or service.
   b. Marketing is the activity, set of institutions, and processes for creating, communicating, delivering, and exchanging offerings that have value for customers, clients, partners, and society at large.
   c. Marketing is the sale of a product or service.
   d. Marketing is the purchase of goods and services.

2. Beyond the traditional "make the sale" model, today's marketing is also about:
   a. market share.
   b. winning marketing awards for best advertisement.
   c. having the best ad agency work on your campaign.
   d. understanding customer needs and delivering value.

3. According to Peter Ducker, if you have great marketing:
   a. you don't have to sell.
   b. the product will fit the customer.
   c. you as a marketer have taken the time to understand your customer.
   d. you will have a great operations and HR team.

4. Beyond the sale, the cumulative function of marketing is
   a. to sell more products and services to consumers.
   b. to communicate and deliver value to, and create value for, the customer.
   c. to create enough public relations buzz so that your product or service gets noticed.
   d. to follow the purchasing behaviour of your consumer.

5. Many marketing professionals would agree that marketing giants like Coke have managed to sustain themselves for so long because:
   a. they are very competitive against category competitors.
   b. they have the best ad campaigns versus their competition.
   c. they have been able to stay on top of consumer trends and what customers love.
   d. they have figured out the right product ingredients for their beverages.

 Apply...

1. In groups, answer the following. Based on the definition of marketing (i.e., that *marketing is the activity, set of institutions, and processes for creating, communicating, delivering, and exchanging offerings that have value for customers, clients, partners and society at large"*), do you believe Coke fulfills all the requirements presented in the definition? Go online and find examples of Coke's marketing to present and support your argument in class.

    _____

    _____

    _____

    _____

    _____

    _____

    _____

    _____

    _____

    _____

    _____

    _____

    _____

    _____

2. Answer the following individually. What organizations have you recently purchased from which you feel have done a great job in marketing their product? Why is that so? Does the organization fulfill the requirements of the definition of marketing? If so how? How much did this company spend on market-ing in the last five years? (Hint: If it was a publicly traded company, you could find its financial statements online—if they are not, you won't be able to.) Present your findings to class.

    _____

    _____

    _____

    _____

    _____

    _____

    _____

    _____

    _____

The Marketing Process

L02 Outline the steps of the marketing process

The **marketing process** is a simple five-step model that is used by organizations to understand how to *create valuable relationships for customers*, as well as to generate *profits for the organization*. The process revolves around consumers, and by creating value for them organizations will reap the rewards in the form of sales, profits, referrals, and long-term customer loyalty (Figure 1).

1. **Stage 1:** Before marketing a product or service to consumers, marketers need to understand the marketplace and the needs and wants of their customers.

2. **Stage 2:** Marketers design a customer-driven marketing strategy with the goal of getting, keeping, and growing their target or "best fit" customers.

3. **Stage 3:** Marketers need to construct a marketing program and plan that delivers superior and differentiated value to consumers.

4. **Stage 4:** Stages 1 to 3 come together at this point to create "customer delight" and a bonding relationship with the customer.

5. **Stage 5:** The organization reaps the rewards of strong customer relationships by capturing value from customers.

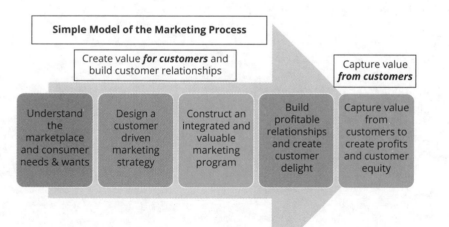

FIGURE 1 Simple model of the marketing process.

Source: Based on Kotler, A., Buchwitz, T. (2017). *Marketing An Introduction,* Chapter 1. Pearson Canada; p. 7.

Practice...

1. In stage 1 of the marketing process,
   a. marketers need to understand the market they are working in.
   b. marketers need to identify the best customers.
   c. marketers need to develop a strategy that will best suit the needs of their consumers.
   d. marketers are focused on building relationships that delight their customers.

2. In stage 2 of the marketing process,
   a. marketers need to understand the market they are working in.
   b. marketers need to identify the best customers.
   c. marketers need to develop a strategy that will best suit the needs of their consumers.
   d. marketers are focused on building relationships that delight their customers.

3. In stage 3 of the marketing process,
   a. marketers need to understand the market they are working in.
   b. marketers need to identify the best customers.
   c. marketers need to develop a strategy that will best suit the needs of their consumers.
   d. marketers are focused on building relationships that delight their customers.

4. In stage 4 of the marketing process,
   a. marketers need to understand the market they are working in.
   b. marketers need to identify the best customers.
   c. marketers need to develop a strategy that will best suit the needs of their consumers.
   d. marketers are focused on building relationships that delight their customers.

5. The first four stages of marketing process are all about:
   a. making a return on investment.
   b. capturing value from customers.
   c. creating value for customers.
   d. building a strong case for future business.

 # Apply...

1. In groups, answer the following. You are the marketing manager for Sharpie Permanent Markers (http://www.sharpie.com/en-CA). Present to the class the first four steps of the marketing process and how you believe Sharpie adds value for consumers.

_____
_____
_____
_____
_____
_____
_____
_____
_____
_____
_____
_____
_____
_____
_____
_____
_____
_____
_____
_____
_____
_____
_____
_____
_____
_____
_____
_____

to be continued

 **Apply…**

continued

2. Explain how Samsung or Apple would employ stage four of the marketing process, creating "customer delight" with regards to their top cell phones? Present your ideas to the class.

_____

_____

_____

_____

_____

_____

_____

_____

_____

_____

_____

_____

_____

_____

_____

_____

_____

_____

_____

The 4 P's … a.k.a. the Marketing Mix

L03 Identify and define the 4Ps that make up the marketing mix

The Four P's (4P's)

Marketing is made up of four elements: *product*, *place*, *promotion*, and *price*. These four elements are also known as the **marketing mix** and are the points of contact between consumers and the marketer's product or service. When planning, a marketer will ask some questions, then assess the strength of the 4Ps and their relevance to the brand, and then assign a portion of the marketing budget to be spent on each element of the marketing mix (Figure 2).

FIGURE 2 The marketing mix.

1. **Product:**

   What are the tangible or intangible products or services that we offer to consumers?

   These are the attributes (features, functions, benefits, and uses) that are capable of exchange or use; usually a mix of tangible and intangible forms. Thus a product may be an idea, a physical entity (a good), or a service, or any combination of the three. It exists for the purpose of exchange in the satisfaction of individual and organizational objectives. Product assessments can include all tangible and intangible features of a product, such as look, feel, taste, personality, and packaging.

2. **Price:**

   What are consumers willing to pay for my product?

   Price is the amount a consumer pays to acquire a product. It is not only important for the marketer to determine what to charge a consumer to buy a product, but also what it will cost to influence a consumer to purchase and use your product or service.

3. **Place:**

   When will products and services available to consumers, and where will they be available?

   Also known as *distribution*, *place* refers to all the aspects that influence accessibility to your product by consumers. To a marketer, being in the right place at the right time is a big part success in marketing.

4. **Promotion:**

   How do I market my product or service to consumers?

   Promotion or Marketing Communications (MarCom) are coordinated promotional messages and related media used to communicate with a market. Promotion consists of the communication tools or channels that are used to effectively get the company's message out, such as digital media, print, radio, television, direct mail, and personal selling.

Practice...

1. What are the 4Ps in marketing?
    a. Price, procedure, promotion, personal selling
    b. Product, place, price, promotion
    c. People, place, promotion, price
    d. Product, place, price, personal selling

2. The Place allows the marketer to understand:
    a. when the product is made.
    b. where the product is made.
    c. where the product is used by the consumer.
    d. where and when the product is available to be purchased.

3. The 4Ps are also known as the:
    a. Marketing Strategy.
    b. Marketing Mix.
    c. Marketing Myopia.
    d. Marketing Matrix.

4. How I market my product or service to consumers is also known as:
    a. marketing strategy.
    b. marketing relationship.
    c. marketing promotion.
    d. marketing distribution.

5. Price is:
    a. what it cost to assemble your product.
    b. the delivery charge to the consumer.
    c. what consumers are willing to pay for your product or service.
    d. what it costs to purchase the advertising strategy proposed by the marketer.

 # Apply…

1. Break into small groups and create a marketing plan for a product or service of your choosing. Determine the four P's: the product, price, promotion, and place, and then present your plan in class. Try to think of something that consumers would want to spend their hard earned money on! Don't know where to start? Try the Edison award winners: https://tinyurl.com/flextext-edison-awards to come up with some ideas or made market one of the products you see on this site.

to be continued

Apply...

continued

2. You've been hired by Gucci to promote their new line of unisex t-shirts. What promotional activities would you use and why? Be ready to present your strategy in class.

_____

_____

_____

_____

_____

_____

_____

_____

_____

_____

_____

_____

_____

_____

_____

_____

_____

_____

_____

_____

_____

_____

_____

_____

_____

_____

_____

_____

Exchange and Relationships

 LO4 Explain the relationship of exchange and why it is required in marketing

Exchange

You use your Android phone or iPhone to download an app and you pay for it using PayPal.

You see a Facebook advertisement for Starbucks offering Frappuccinos at half price, and you redeem an electronic coupon for your treat.

You watch the news on TV and listen to the views of a political candidate, and on Election Day you vote for that person.

These are examples of **exchanges** and the ultimate outcome for marketing is when a successful exchange occurs.

> *An exchange is the act of obtaining a desired object from someone by offering something in return.* (Armstrong et al., 2017)

Exchange and the Marketing Organization

The process is simple, and it requires an individual or an organization to satisfy the need or want of a consumer by offering its goods or services in exchange for something. Beyond money, consumers may be willing to offer their votes in exchange for the right political candidate, or donate their time to a not-for-profit organization which may be fundraising.

As a marketer, your role is to bring about a response to something that your organization is offering to consumers. You create offers for your products or services that deliver consumer value, as well as an exchange. The more valuable and fulfilling your product experiences are, the more exchanges with consumers you will have and the more meaningful your relationship with your consumer will be. Companies want to build strong relationships with their customers by consistently delivering superior value to their customers.

Exchange and the Consumer

As a consumer, you too must be willing to give up something in order to receive or experience something that you would rather have. For example, you go into a restaurant and order your favourite meal. You eat the food and then you pay for it with your credit card. That's a basic exchange relationship. The response may be more than just buying or trading products or services for money, as stated above. If the service or experience was positive, it is likely that you will return again, pass your praises on to friends or family members, or "like" them on social media.

Most consumers will relinquish something in order to receive a product or service, but in order for the exchange to qualify as successful, there are some basic rules that must be met:

- An exchange is successful, if there are at least *two parties* exchanging something of value to each other.
- An exchange is successful, if both parties *clearly communicate* their intentions.
- An exchange is successful, if both parties *accept the offer and want to engage in a deal with each other*.

In our example, the fast-food restaurant wants your business and will take your money. You freely pay for the food because you are hungry. An exchange may not always be successful. You might really want to buy a sports car, but one of the exchange steps might not occur. For example, you might not have the money to accept the salesperson's offer or the space to securely park your vehicle.

 # Practice...

1. An exchange takes place when:
   a. two people argue over the price of a product.
   b. people give away their product or service.
   c. people give up something to receive something they would rather have.
   d. stores give away samples to consumers, in the hope that consumers will buy at a later date.

2. If marketers create valuable and fulfilling product experiences, they will most likely have:
   a. more exchanges with consumers.
   b. more meaningful experiences with their consumers.
   c. the ability to build a loyal clientele.
   d. more revenue for the company.

3. "An exchange is:
   a. the act of obtaining a desired object from someone by offering something in return."
   b. successful if only the marketer exchanges something of value with the consumer."
   c. successful if only the consumer clearly communicates her intention to purchase a product or service."
   d. always successful, even if you can't afford the product."

4. In order for an exchange to take place, you must have:
   a. a marketer exchanging something of value.
   b. a consumer exchanging something of value.
   c. two parties—a marketer and a consumer exchanging something of value.
   d. a strong marketing strategy and campaign.

Apply...

1. In groups, answer the following. In the competing with the soft drink market, the brand Voss (https://tinyurl.com/flextext-voss) has to deal with lots of competitors. Create three strong offers to consumers that will cause consumers to purchase your bottled water product over other soft drinks or juices. Present your offers in class.

_____

_____

_____

_____

_____

_____

_____

_____

_____

_____

_____

_____

_____

_____

_____

_____

_____

_____

_____

_____

_____

_____

_____

_____

_____

_____

to be continued

Apply...

continued

2. As an iPhone or Samsung Super Fan and early adopter of their products, how much would you be willing to pay in exchange for its newest cell phone? How valuable would the phone's product offering have to be in order to get you to spend top dollar for their product, which could easily be over $1,000.00?

_____

_____

_____

_____

_____

_____

_____

_____

_____

KNOW...

Learning Objectives

1. The definition of marketing and why marketing is important:

   Marketing is the activity, set of institutions, and processes for creating, communicating, delivering, and exchanging offerings that have value for customers, clients, partners and society at large. (American Marketing Association)

   In the end, marketing's central focus is the consumer of a business's product or service.
   Though there are many marketing definitions, as a student of marketing, it is important to appreciate that the term "marketing" means different things to different people.

2. The marketing process:

   The marketing process is a simple five-step model that is used by organizations to understand how to *create valuable relationships for customers*, as well as *profits for the organization*. The process revolves around the consumer, and, by creating value for consumers, organizations will reap the rewards in the form of sales, profits, referrals, and long-term customer loyalty.

3. The 4Ps of marketing. Also known as the Marketing Mix:

   Marketing's four elements of *product*, *place*, *price*, and *promotion* are the core of a company's marketing plan. These elements must all be focused on the final consumer. Companies want to provide a long-term, supportive relationship and bring value to the consumer. Marketers have to understand the importance of focusing on the customer.

4. The value and purpose of exchange in order for marketing to take place:

   The ultimate goal of a marketer is to complete a successful *exchange*. There must be at least two parties, and each party must have something of value to offer the other. The parties must be capable of delivering value and be able to accept the offer. Finally, in order for an exchange to take place, each party must want to deal with the other party. Marketing is about understanding customers and finding ways to provide products or services which they demand.

Key Terms

Exchange: The act of obtaining a desired object from someone by offering something in return.

Marketing: It is a value-laden exchange between an organization and its customers.

Marketing Process: A simple five-step model that is used by organizations to understand how to create valuable relationships for customers, as well as profit for the organization.

The Marketing Mix (the 4Ps): *product*, *place*, *promotion*, and *price*. These four elements are also known as the marketing mix and are the points of contact between consumers and the marketer's product or service.

Answers to Practice

What Is Marketing?
1. b   2. d   3. c   4. b   5. c

The Marketing Process
1. a   2. c   3. c   4. d   5. c

The 4 P's . . . a.k.a. the Marketing Mix
1. b   2. c   3. b   4. c   5. c

Exchange and Relationships
1. c   2. c   3. a   4. c

References

Armstrong, Gary, Kotler, Philip, Marketing: An Introduction, 13th Ed., ©2017. Reprinted and Electronically reproduced by permission of Pearson Education, Inc., New York, NY.

American Marketing Association's Online Marketing Dictionary.

Drucker on Marketing: Lessons from the World's Most Influential Business Thinker, William A. Cohen, Mc Graw Hill, 2012.

Kotler, A. & Buchwitz, T. (2017). Marketing an Introduction, Chapter 1. Pearson Canada; p. 7.

Stengel, J. (December 12, 2013). Things every brand can learn from Coke. *Forbes Magazine*, 10. Retrieved from https://www.forbes.com/sites/jimstengel/2013/12/12/10-things-every-brand-can-learn-from-coke/#dc1e373493e1

2 Marketing Management

LEARNING OBJECTIVES

LO1 Define what a market is and why it is important to assess the market before commencing with a marketing plan

LO2 Understand the meaning and importance of marketing management

LO3 Learn the difference between marketing, production, product, sales, and societal marketing orientations and how one can affect a company's financial success

LO4 Define product orientation

LO5 Define sales orientation

LO6 Define marketing orientation

LO7 Define societal marketing orientation

LEARN...

The one thing every organization (either on the profit or not-for-profit side of the fence) needs to do is build relationships with customers. That is, they should seek out the loyalty of the best and most tenured customers and grab the attention and interest of those entering the market. These relationships are asserted on one simple premise—without customers, an organization will not exist.

Though there may not be a universally accepted definition of marketing, there is a consistent premise across most marketing definitions that "the customer is king" and the most vital contributor to the organization.

If today's businesses exist to serve their customer first, then it is the marketing manager's main role to assess the market and the customers that have the potential "to be king" and then design strategies that will deliver them value. This customer value will yield a satisfied customer who keeps coming back for more and ultimately profit the organization.

It is up to the marketing manager to assess the market first and then develop a *marketing management* platform that is premised on a marketing, product, production, sales, or societal marketing orientation. The marketing manager then implements strategic marketing initiatives for the organization.

These initiatives should attract new customers and retain (as well as) increase the value of existing customers. Tasks include performing market research, developing pricing strategies, and coordinating relevant staff and vendors (marketing, creative, media, and agencies) to meet firm's objectives.

What Is a Market?

L01 Define what a market is and why it is important to assess the market before commencing with a marketing plan

A marketer's objective is to design strategies that will build strong and profitable relationships with consumers. In order to achieve this objective, the marketer will first need to assess the market in which the product or service exists.

What is a market? According to Armstrong et al. (2017),

> *a market is the set of all actual and potential buyers of a product or service.*

As a vital contributor of the production of a product or service, the marketer's role has traditionally been to research the market and to manage the relationships that the marketer's company has with its customers. Given today's tech-savvy audience, consumers are now redefining the concept of market and are marketing to other consumers, as well as to the marketing organization.

Digital technologies, like mobile phone apps, social media, and the internet, have allowed consumers to research information, make decisions, influence others, and provide feedback and commentary from their various electronic devices. Marketers today are not only asking how they can influence the market, but how the market (that is, consumers) can influence them as well.

Figure 1 demonstrates that there are many intermediaries that a marketer will face before reaching the market of final consumers. Each intermediary in the **modern marketing system** will be affected by major environmental forces, such as technology, politics, culture, nature, and society at large. To add to that, today's consumer market is able to talk back to marketers and suppliers and affect the traditional marketing flow and process.

Today, consumers have direct contact with brands (via Twitter, Facebook, Instagram, etc.) and solutions to questions and problems can therefore be quickly solved and alleviated.

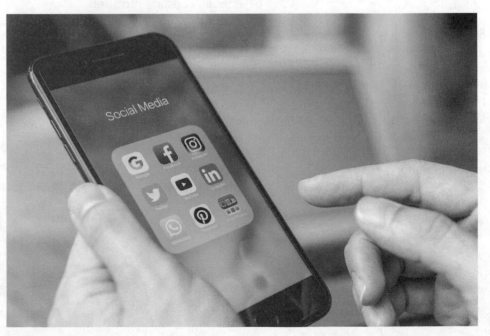

Source: Vasin Lee/Shutterstock.

Companies can look at their internal strengths and then adopt one of five orientations: production, product, sales, marketing, and societal marketing, which in the long run will be the voice of the brand and will help to differentiate the organization from its competitors. These activities and philosophies apply to almost all types of organizations, whether profit-making or not-for-profit.

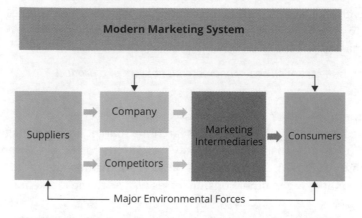

FIGURE 1 The modern marketing system.

Source: Based on Armstrong, Kotler, Trifts, Buchwitz, Marketing An Introduction, Pearson Canada, 2017.

Practice...

1. A market is:
   a. a place where merchants sell products to consumers.
   b. the set of all actual and potential buyers of a product or service.
   c. a brick and mortar location available to consumers.
   d. a place where consumers can shop for products.

2. A marketer's primary objective is:
   a. to liaise with the accounting, finance, and budget department.
   b. to test products before they are introduced into the market.
   c. to design strategies that will build strong and profitable relationships with consumers.
   d. to find the right and proper endorser for a product.

3. Marketers today are not only asking how they can influence the market but how the market (that is, consumers) can influence them as well.
   a. True
   b. False

4. The modern marketing system:
   a. disregards environmental factors.
   b. is totally consumer focused.
   c. is all about cutting costs and distributing products only to those that warrant them.
   d. acknowledges consumers' feedback and the environmental factors that influence consumers.

5. The modern marketing system is affected by:
   a. price.
   b. product.
   c. place.
   d. intermediaries.

Apply...

1. Go to the social media platform Facebook and review posts from a company you like such as Apple, H&M, Sport Chek, or Sephora (if there is another retailer you like, go to their page). How does the retailer interact with their customers? Does the retailer provide value on their Facebook page? If so, how do they do that? Can you influence the retailer via their Facebook page? If so, how? Give an example.

_____

_____

_____

_____

_____

_____

_____

_____

_____

_____

_____

_____

2. Create a mind map. In the middle, start with a web site you purchase stuff from. Working from that center point, identify all the intermediaries involved with your online purchase. Present those intermediaries in class, explaining how the goods get to you.

_____

_____

_____

_____

_____

_____

_____

_____

_____

_____

_____

_____

_____

What Is Marketing Management?

L02 Understand the meaning and importance of marketing management

After an analysis of various market intermediaries, a marketer needs to chalk out the philosophy or strategy that will guide the organization, build its brand, and (hopefully) form a profitable relationship with customers. This process is known as **marketing management**.

According to Kotler and Keller (2008),

> *marketing management is 'the art and science of choosing target markets and getting, keeping, and growing customers through creating, delivering, and communicating superior customer value'.* (p. 5)

Armstrong et al. (2017) define marketing management as:

> *the art and science of choosing target markets and building profitable relationships with them.*

Why Is Marketing Management Important?

A marketing manager is responsible for developing and implementing strategic marketing initiatives for a business or business unit. These initiatives are designed to attract new customers, increase the value of retained customers, guide the brand, and represent the organization to consumers. Without customers, there would be no business.

Some of the tasks of the marketing management team include:

- performing consumer market research,
- performing competitive market research,
- introducing new products to the market,
- increasing or decreasing the production of existing products,
- developing pricing strategies,
- assessing distribution costs and strategies,
- developing internal communications strategies,
- developing external communications strategies,
- coordinating the relevant internal staff, and
- coordinating external partners (advertising, marketing, creative and media, and agencies).

To sum up, marketing management may be defined as the division within an organization that plans, implements, and controls the marketing of an organization.

Practice...

1. Marketing management is:
   a. the analysis, planning, implementation, and control of programs designed to bring about desired exchanges with target markets for the purpose of achieving organizational objectives.
   b. the team in charge of the marketing campaign.
   c. the art and science of choosing target markets and building profitable relationships with them.
   d. the management team in charge of the marketing department

2. Some of the tasks that the marketing management team are not responsible for include:
   a. developing pricing strategies.
   b. conducting competitive research.
   c. asking consumers what they think and like about a product.
   d. presenting financial forecasts and corporate budgets to management.

3. One of the many tasks that marketing managers are responsible for include:
   a. liaising with the competition.
   b. attracting customers who will not spend time with or money on the brand.
   c. decreasing the value of retained customers.
   d. developing internal communications strategies for the organization.

4. The process of chalking out a management philosophy that will guide the organization and build a profitable relationship that customers are attracted to is known as:
   a. the sales orientation.
   b. marketing management.
   c. the marketing orientation.
   d. relationship marketing.

Apply...

1. Go to the "Frank And Oak" website (https://ca.frankandoak.com/) and review their site. What are some strategic marketing initiatives the marketing manager incorporated onto the web site?

_____

_____

_____

_____

_____

_____

_____

_____

_____

to be continued

 # Apply...

continued

2. The responsibility of a marketing manager is to "chalk out the philosophy or strategy that will guide the organization, build its brand, and (hopefully) form a profitable relationship with customers". Pick two retailers you like to patronize (go to their web site, if you have to) and explain to the class how these companies build their *brand* and develop their *own philosophy*. Can't think of anyone? Go to Patagonia's website (http://www.patagonia.ca/) or Starbucks website (https://www.starbucks.ca/) to view how they build their brand and philosophy.

_____

_____

_____

_____

_____

_____

_____

_____

_____

_____

_____

_____

_____

_____

_____

_____

_____

_____

_____

_____

_____

_____

_____

_____

Selecting the Right Marketing Philosophy

L03 Learn the difference between marketing, production, product, sales, and societal marketing orientations and how one can affect a company's financial success

L04 Define production orientation

There are five marketing concepts that organizations adopt and execute. The marketing department of an organization designs strategies that build profitable relationships with target consumers. But what philosophy is the best for a company in setting marketing strategies?

How Does a Company Choose Its Sales and Marketing Philosophy?

A company will select its philosophy by deciding how to harness its internal strengths to reach out to consumers. Companies adopt one of the five concepts when deciding on how to create an organizational marketing process. These concepts (Figure 2) are:

1. Production

2. Product

3. Sales

4. Marketing

5. Societal Marketing

Production Orientation

When McDonald's first opened its first restaurant in the Soviet Union, people were willing to wait hours in the cold for a Big Mac. The product wasn't any different than what you would find in other McDonald's around the world, but what was different was the restaurant's focus on customer service and providing customers with a consistent restaurant experience. This was something that the restaurant chain was praised and lauded for, and something that Russian consumers had not been used to in their restaurant dining experiences.

FIGURE 2 The organizational marketing process and its concepts.

Production orientation is one of the oldest orientations and a philosophy that focuses on the strengths and capabilities of the firm producing products it wants, rather than producing products that are based on the desires and needs of the consumer.

It holds that consumers will favour the organization's highly available and affordable products, and hence focus on producing more of that particular product—only. On top of their production focus, companies with this philosophy look not only to produce more, but also look at ways to further improve their distribution and get their products to consumers.

The one problem with production orientated companies is that they do not take into consideration how their products suit customers' needs to the same degree as companies that are market or sales oriented. Production orientated companies tend to ignore their customers' needs and focus only on efficiently building a "better mousetrap" that their customers will come to them for.

An easy way to understand this orientation is to reference Henry Ford, the original manufacturer of American cars. Ford created one type of car and stated that the consumer could have it in only one colour—black. This was irrespective of the perspective of the consumer. If a car manufacturer kept that philosophy today and controlled the options available to their consumers, they would be out of business very quickly!

Practice...

1. The five marketing concepts are:
   a. production, promotion, sales, marketing, and social marketing.
   b. production, promotion, price, marketing, and social marketing.
   c. production, product, sales, marketing, and social marketing.
   d. promotion, sales, management, marketing, and social marketing.

2. The statement that best characterizes production orientation is:
   a. A philosophy that focuses on aggressive sales techniques.
   b. A philosophy that focuses on the internal capabilities of the firm rather than on the desires and needs of the marketplace.
   c. A philosophy that uses marketing as its main premise.
   d. A philosophy that focuses on the consumers, competitors, and marketers.

3. An example of a production-oriented company is:
   a. Disney.
   b. Apple.
   c. Coca-Cola.
   d. The old Ford Motor Company

4. Production-based companies . . .
   a. provide a variety of products to their consumers.
   b. only build products that they want to build.
   c. are focussed on customer service first.
   d. research the market before releasing their product.

 # Apply...

1. The majority of fast-food restaurants are considered production-based organizations. Choosing two fast-food companies, list several products that each company offers to consumers that are considered "production based".

    _____
    _____
    _____
    _____
    _____
    _____
    _____
    _____
    _____
    _____
    _____
    _____
    _____
    _____
    _____
    _____
    _____
    _____

2. Should Walmart be considered a production based company? Why or why not?

    _____
    _____
    _____
    _____
    _____
    _____
    _____
    _____
    _____
    _____
    _____
    _____
    _____
    _____
    _____

Selecting the Right Marketing Philosophy: Product Orientation

L04 Define product orientation

Product Orientation

Product orientation is a philosophy that was incorporated in the 1920s when there was no sophistication in product development, and companies solely focused on developing and delivering a high-quality product. This philosophy holds that a consumer will favour products from a brand that offers the most in quality, performance, and innovation. The fundamental tools of product orientation include research, product development, and product focus.

Hence, a product-oriented company looks at producing quality products and fixing them at the right price so that the consumer will differentiate the company's products from its competitors' and purchase them. Marketing strategies are focused on making continuous product improvements and reinforcing news of those improvements with customers.

One problem associated with the product concept is that it may lead to marketing myopia. Targeting only on the company's products and not the wants and needs of consumers could lead to a disconnect and a decrease in market share. Thus, companies need to take innovations and features seriously and provide only those which the customer needs.

An example of a successful product-oriented company is Gillette. The Gillette Company focuses on producing the best possible disposable razors and shaving products in the market. Thereby, they distinguish their products with a high-quality razor blade, ease of use, and the right pricing strategy.

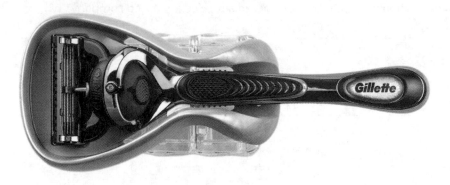

Source: Bborriss.67/Shutterstock.

A product-oriented company that saw great early success is Sony. The creation of its Walkman proved to be successful but was not based on what customers wanted at that time. As consumer needs for music and audio devices changed, the Walkman was not able to maintain its level of success.

Source: Ned Snowman/Shutterstock

Practice...

1. Product orientation focuses on:
   a. producing "one of a kind" products.
   b. delivering a high-quality product.
   c. pitching and selling products to consumers.
   d. the environmental and social impact of products.

2. The marketing focus of a product-orientation firm is:
   a. to assess the optimal distribution channels to promote the product.
   b. reach out to consumers and ask what they're willing to pay for goods and services.
   c. to sell the products that the firm wants to sell.
   d. to make continuous product improvements and reinforcing news of those improvements with customers.

3. Consumers who subscribe to product orientation:
   a. will favour products from a brand that offers the most in quality, performance, and innovation.
   b. will favour products from a brand that takes the time to get to know them better.
   c. will favour products from a brand that is relationship-based.
   d. will favour brands that sell products to consumers.

4. The Gillette razor company is an example of a company with a product marketing orientation.
   a. True
   b. False

 **Apply...**

1. Is product-oriented strategy employed by cell phone manufacturers like Apple or Samsung? If so, do either of these companies unknowingly employ elements of marketing myopia in their strategic planning? If so, how does this happen?

_____

_____

_____

_____

_____

_____

_____

_____

_____

_____

_____

_____

_____

2. In production orientation, marketing strategies are focused on making continuous product improvements and reinforcing news of those improvements with customers. Aside from cell phones, think of another industry that does this. Provide the class with an example of a company and be able to justify to the class why you believe the company you picked is "production oriented".

_____

_____

_____

_____

_____

_____

_____

_____

_____

_____

_____

_____

_____

Selecting the Right Marketing Philosophy: Sales Orientation

LO5 Define sales orientation

The selling concept is the idea that *"consumers will not buy enough of the firm's products unless it undertakes a large-scale selling and promotion effort"* (Armstrong et al., 2017).

Sales Orientation: The company believes that it will sell more products or services, if very aggressive sales methods are used to gain higher sales. Sales-oriented companies rely heavily on promotion and a highly trained aggressive sales force.

The marketing management team focuses on creating sales transactions, rather than on building long-term, profitable customer relationships. In other words, the aim is to sell what the company makes and has to offer, rather than making what the market wants. Leaders in this industry are good at tracking down customer leads and have an aggressive sales force network that promotes the product's overall benefits to the consumer.

The selling concept is typically practiced by companies that sell goods and services to other companies that consumers do not frequently purchase or normally don't think of when shopping. These products can include burial plots, caskets, and insurance. Another example would be a door-to-door salesman selling vacuum cleaners or a lotion salesman at a mall kiosk.

Again, the problem with this type of philosophy is that it is profit driven rather than relationship driven and, again, does not focus on what the customer and market requires, but rather is too caught up in pushing products or services with a polished sales technique. The marketing management team assumes that customers who have been persuaded to buy its product will like it. If they don't like it, they will possibly forget their disappointment and buy it again later.

Kiosks such as this though product laden, are more focused on selling their products or services rather than addressing what customers want.

Source: Leungchopan/Shutterstock.

Practice...

1. The selling concept holds the idea that:
   a. consumers will not buy enough of the firm's products unless it undertakes a large-scale selling and promotion effort.
   b. an aggressive sales force is required in order to push the product forward to consumers.
   c. heavy promotion force will get product across to consumers.
   d. the product will sell quicker, if there is a strong advertising campaign attached to it.

2. Sales orientation is:
   a. based on the idea that firms use their internal strengths.
   b. based on the idea that people will buy more goods and services, if aggressive sales techniques are used.
   c. based on the idea that, when a company uses multiple marketing channels, it will help to raise more awareness.
   d. based on the idea that firms care about creating customer value.

3. Which type of orientation is used if a company relies on aggressive techniques to persuade consumers to purchase its products?
   a. Sales orientation
   b. Production orientation
   c. Marketing orientation
   d. Societal marketing orientation

4. A life insurance company would most likely use a _____ approach when marketing.
   a. sales orientation
   b. production orientation
   c. marketing orientation
   d. societal marketing orientation

5. The main problem with the sales orientation philosophy is that:
   a. the techniques of sales reps tend to be very aggressive.
   b. there is no variety in the product offerings of the sales rep.
   c. it only focuses on selling business-to-business products rather than business to consumer products.
   d. it does not focus on what the customer and the market require.

 # Apply...

1. Would Vivint (https://www.vivint.com/) be considered a company who employs a sales orientation strategy? Be able to support your position with a couple of facts.

_____

_____

_____

_____

_____

_____

_____

_____

2. Do real estate companies such as Remax (https://www.remax.ca/) or Prudential (http://www.prudential. ca/) use a sales orientation strategy? Explain your position.

_____

_____

_____

_____

_____

_____

_____

_____

_____

_____

_____

_____

_____

_____

_____

_____

_____

_____

_____

_____

_____

Selecting the Right Marketing Philosophy: Marketing Orientation

L06 Define marketing orientation

Marketing orientation is the first philosophy to adopt a "customer first" approach and take into account the importance of the customer's needs. The organization believes that it exists to satisfy a consumer's wants and needs, while also providing shareholder and corporate benefit.

Under the marketing concept, customer focus and value are the routes to achieve sales and profits. The role of the marketing team is not to find the right customers for their products, but the right products for their customers. Marketers need to make their brand so strong and appealing that customers prefer it over every other competitor in the market. By researching the customer's needs and wants, as well as their purchasing behaviour, brands and companies can build *long-term relationships with their customers* that will allow them to return to a brand or product when it suits them.

Examples of businesses that are known for following this philosophy are Apple, Google, Disney, Amazon, and Coca-Cola. They keep their eyes on their consumers at all times and create products and services that best suit both their existing customers and new customers entering the market. The Figure 3 below shows that among the leading global brands, marketing-oriented companies tend to dominate the chart.

Of the top 10 global brands of 2017, the majority follow the marketing orientation philosophy.

Rank				Brand Value (USD $ Millions)		Brand rating	
2017	2016	Name	Country	2017	2016	2017	2016
1 ⬆	2	Google		109,470	88,173	AAA+	AAA+
2 ⬇	1	Apple		107,141	145,918	AAA	AAA
3 ➡	3	Amazon.com		106,396	69,642	AAA-	AA+
4 ⬆	6	AT&T		87,016	59,904	AAA	AA+
5 ⬇	4	Microsoft		76,265	67,258	AAA	AAA
6 ⬆	7	Samsung Group		66,219	58,619	AAA-	AAA
7 ⬇	5	Verizon		65,875	63,116	AAA-	AAA-
8 ➡	8	Walmart		62,211	53,657	AA+	AA
9 ⬆	17	Facebook		61,998	34,002	AAA	AAA-
10 ⬆	13	ICBC		47,832	36,334	AAA	AA+

FIGURE 3 2017 Leading global brands.

Source: Top to most valuable Global Brand of 2017, In Brand Finance Global 500, February 2017. Copyright © 2017 by Brand Finance PLC. Used by permission.

Practice...

1. Marketing orientation firms focus mostly on:
    a. short-term relationships with customers.
    b. long-term relationships with customers.
    c. enhancing their existing product.
    d. offering their product to consumers at the lowest possible price.

2. Analyze the importance of marketing orientation.
    a. A firm focuses on the internal capabilities of the firm, rather than on the desires and needs of the marketplace.
    b. A firm obtains information about customers, competitors, and markets and delivers superior customer value to customers.
    c. A firm uses marketing techniques such as social media to help promote the company.
    d. A firm uses aggressive sales techniques.

3. Marketing orientation:
    a. tries to build a better mousetrap.
    b. takes a "customer first" approach.
    c. looks at the company's internal strengths to further enhance the product offering to consumers.
    d. focuses on selling products and services to consumers.

4. The role of the marketing-oriented marketing team is to:
    a. aggressively sell the right customers a product.
    b. aggressively sell the right products to customers.
    c. find the right customers for its product.
    d. find the right products for its customers.

Apply...

1. Conduct online research to find three techniques used by the Disney Corporation to better market its product to consumers. Present your findings to the class.

_____

_____

_____

_____

_____

_____

_____

_____

_____

_____

_____

_____

_____

_____

_____

_____

_____

_____

_____

_____

_____

2. In a group, produce a list of the approaches that you would take as a marketing-orientated organization to better promote your academic institution. Present your strategies to the class.

_____

_____

_____

_____

_____

_____

_____

_____

_____

_____

_____

Selecting the Right Marketing Philosophy: Societal Marketing Orientation

L07 Define societal marketing orientation

Societal marketing orientation places emphasis on the long-term well-being of society as a whole. While traditional product and service marketing is still a key function of this type of marketing plan, the focal point of societal marketing is *society*. The concept holds that, according to Armstrong et al. (2017),

> *marketing strategy should deliver value to customers in a way that maintains or improves both the consumer's and society's well-being.*

It calls for sustainable marketing, and marketing that is socially and environmentally responsible that meets the present needs of consumers and businesses. It calls for all of this while also preserving or enhancing the ability of future generations to meet their needs.

Companies that endorse this idea follow the marketing orientation; in addition, they reinforce in their marketing that their product or service protects or enhances society's interests. This concept takes the idea of providing customer value to the next level and looks to balance three considerations when setting their marketing strategies: company profits, consumer wants, and society's interests (Figure 4).

Many companies are slowly either fully or partially trying to implement the societal marketing concept. A current example is the explosive growth of green products that companies market. Companies like Whole Foods and lululemon promote the idea that their products are helpful to consumers, good for company profits, and also better the environment. The clothing manufacturer Patagonia encourages consumers not to buy things they don't need and encourages customers to repair rather than replace their products. Their commitment lies in their products—not just their messaging and marketing. Wetsuits are made of natural rubber and plastic bottles are turned into parkas. Patagonia also recognizes the importance of political action on the environment and has made voting for eco-friendly leaders a cornerstone of its sustainability message.

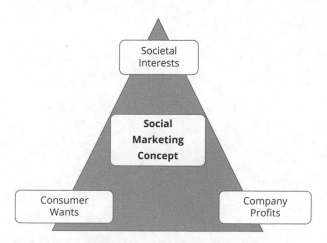

FIGURE 4 Considerations underlying the societal marketing concept.

Source: Based on Armstrong, Kotler, Trifts, Buchwitz, Marketing An Introduction, Pearson Canada, 2017.

Practice...

1. Societal marketing questions whether the marketing concept overlooks:
   a. the sales channel.
   b. consumer demand.
   c. consumer wants versus welfare.
   d. the development of product.

2. What is societal marketing orientation?
   a. It is a combination of marketing orientation plus the addition of being concerned about society's best interests.
   b. It refers to a company that only cares about society as a whole and not just the consumer.
   c. It refers to a company that markets its product to consumers.
   d. It refers to a company that only makes products for charity.

3. An example of a North American auto manufacturing firm that best uses the societal marketing approach is:
   a. General Motors.
   b. Ford.
   c. Tesla.
   d. Chrysler.

4. The societal marketing approach looks to balance three considerations when setting marketing strategies for them. They are:
   a. consumer wants, shareholder value, and societal interests.
   b. company profits, consumer wants, and product development.
   c. company profits, consumer wants, and societal interests.
   d. consumer wants, shareholder value, and societal interests.

5. The societal marketing approach is all about human welfare before profits.
   a. True
   b. False

 **Apply...**

1. List three social marketing orientation firms. Present to the class the things that they do from a social perspective that differentiates them from their competitors.

_____
_____
_____
_____
_____
_____
_____
_____
_____
_____
_____
_____
_____
_____
_____
_____
_____
_____
_____
_____
_____
_____
_____
_____
_____
_____
_____
_____
_____
_____
_____
_____
_____
_____
_____
_____

to be continued

 # Apply...

continued

2. List the things that you would do as a marketer to make your financial services institution (bank or credit union) a better social marketer.

_____

_____

_____

_____

_____

_____

_____

_____

_____

_____

_____

_____

_____

_____

_____

_____

_____

_____

_____

_____

KNOW...

Learning Objectives

1. A marketer's objective is to design strategies that will build strong and profitable relationships with consumers. In order to achieve this objective, the marketer will first need to assess the market in which the product or service exists. Without a market, marketing and the firms that they market for do not exist.

2. Marketing management may be defined as the division within an organization that plans, implements, and controls the marketing of an organization.

3. There are five marketing concepts that organizations adopt and execute. The marketing department of an organization designs strategies that build profitable relationships with target consumers. A company will select its philosophy by deciding how to harness its internal strengths to reach out to its consumers.

4-7. Know the five marketing philosophies that companies adopt.

Key Terms

Market: A market is the set of all actual and potential buyers of a product or service.

Marketing Management: Marketing management is the analysis, planning, implementation, and control of programs designed to bring about desired exchanges with target markets for the purpose of achieving organizational objectives.

Marketing Orientation: Marketing orientation adopts a "customer first" approach and takes into account the importance of the customer's needs. The organization believes that it exists to satisfy consumer's wants and needs and also provides shareholder and corporate benefit.

Modern Marketing System: There are many intermediaries that a marketer will face before reaching the market of final consumers. Each intermediary in the system will be affected by major environmental forces such as technology, politics, culture, nature, and society at large. To add to that, the consumer market today is able to talk back to marketers and suppliers and affect the traditional marketing flow and process.

Product Orientation: A product-oriented company looks mostly at producing quality products and fixing them at the right price so that the consumer differentiates the company's products and purchases it.

Production Orientation: Product orientation holds that consumers will favour the organization's highly available and affordable products and hence focus on producing more of that particular product—only.

Sales Orientation: The company believes that it will sell more product or services, if very aggressive sales methods are used to gain higher sales. Sales-oriented companies rely heavily on promotion and a highly trained aggressive sales force.

Societal Marketing Orientation: The societal marketing concept ranks human welfare ahead of profits and satisfying the consumer's wants. The concept holds that "marketing strategy should deliver value to customers in a way that maintains or improves both the consumer's and society's well-being".

Answers to Practice

What Is a Market?
1. b   2. c   3. a   4. d   5. d

What Is Marketing Management?
1. a   2. d   3. d   4. b

Selecting the Right Marketing Philosophy
1. c   2. b   3. d   4. b

Selecting the Right Marketing Philosophy: Product Orientation
1. b   2. d   3. a   4. a

Selecting the Right Marketing Philosophy: Sales Orientation

1. b   2. b   3. a   4. a   5. d

Selecting the Right Marketing Philosophy: Marketing Orientation

1. b   2. b   3. b   4. d

Selecting the Right Marketing Philosophy: Societal Marketing Orientation

1. c   2. a   3. c   4. c   5. b

References

Armstrong, Gary, Kotler, Philip, Marketing: An Introduction, 13th Ed., ©2017. Reprinted and Electronically reproduced by permission of Pearson Education, Inc., New York, NY.

Armstrong, Kotler, Trifts, Buchwitz, Marketing An Introduction, Pearson Canada, 2017.

Kotler & Keller. (2008). *Marketing Management* (13th Edition). Pearson; 2008, page 5.

3 Creating Customer Value

LEARNING OBJECTIVES

 L01 Learn how to recognize a sales-oriented marketing strategy, including what types of goods and services are typically sold using this strategy and what promotional techniques go along with it

 L02 Learn how to recognize a marketing-oriented marketing strategy, including what types of goods and services are typically sold using this strategy and what promotional techniques go along with it

 L03 Define and understand the types of customer value

L04 Understand how customer satisfaction leads to stronger customer relationships

L05 Learn what relationship marketing is as well as look at some related strategies

LEARN...

Everyone knows what is meant by the *price* of a product.

But just as important as a product's price is its *value* to the customer.

To some customers, *value means price*—as in *what is the value of this car?*

And to other customers, *value means benefit*—as in *the value I get from this car is great gas mileage* and a *0–60 km/h speed in under 4 seconds*.

What a customer pays for a product is not only the price in the form of cash, cheque, credit, or interest but also a non-financial price such as time, effort, service, an enhanced image, or even a smile on one's face. It is also this type of satisfaction that marketers need to be aware of.

Customers look for value in the brands and companies they choose to do business with. And it is just as important for marketers to understand this value and to come up with the right strategy that will best attract and retain its customers. The following chapter will help you to understand the strategies and lengths that marketers go through to build a valuable brand and long-term relationships with their customers.

The Organization's Focus—Marketing Oriented or Sales Oriented? Sales Oriented

LO1 Learn how to recognize a sales-oriented marketing strategy, including what types of goods and services are typically sold using this strategy and what promotional techniques go along with it

Have you ever wondered why Timothy's or the Second Cup Coffee Company have slowly fallen out of popularity and why brands like Tim Horton's and Starbucks' have grown? Or why Netflix took down Rogers *Shomi* and now rules the entertainment and video streaming airwaves? Last but not least, why did the smartphone company RIM (makers of the Blackberry or "Crackberry" smartphone) fall out of popularity and why did Apple's iPhone and Samsung's Galaxy grow in success?

The answer may lie within the marketing direction that these organizations decided to take on. Was its marketing direction sales-oriented or marketing-oriented?

The main differences between a sales-oriented company and a marketing-oriented company have to do with their overall view of the marketplace and the strategy they take on.

A **sales-oriented company** is very internally focused and looks to sell products to the market that they are successful at making. These companies are primarily focused on selling their products to their consumers and at times pay little attention to other areas of marketing such as research or surveying for customer appreciation. They believe that a high sales volume will generate high profits for the organization. These beliefs may cause them to miss opportunities to better serve their customer base. A company that uses a sales-oriented marketing strategy makes the following assumptions regarding their customers:

- Everyone is a potential customer.

- Their customers do not want to spend their dollars to buy what the company has to offer.

- Their customers will buy more products and services, if they use aggressive sales techniques in order to persuade them to buy.

- High sales volumes equal high profits for the company.

Companies that use a sales-oriented marketing strategy primarily use two types of promotion to communicate with their customers: *advertising* to make potential customers aware of what they have to offer and *personal selling* either door-to-door or through telemarketing, to get potential customers to take action and buy their products and services.

A sales-oriented strategy differs from a market-oriented strategy in the following ways:

- They focus on selling what the company makes, not necessarily what the customer wants.

- They pay very little attention to the changing needs of their customers or to the changes that take place in the marketplace.

- They put a higher premium on short-term, one-off sales than on having a long-term relationship with their customers.

- The focus of their marketing message is on quality and price rather than the brand benefits and its impact on the consumer.

Examples of sales-oriented companies include large furniture retailers like the Brick and Leons, Dell Computers, Rogers, and large pharmaceutical companies like Johnson & Johnson, Pfizer, and Merck.

Recently the Dell computer company has tried to evolve into a full-service business-solutions provider but is still known by consumers as a marketer of consumer tech devices such as PCs, servers, and tablets.

Source: Ymgerman/Shutterstock.

Practice...

1. What is the main difference between a sales-oriented company and a marketing-oriented company?
    a. One gives away product while the other company makes the customer pay.
    b. It is the amount of money invested in the company.
    c. It has to do with how they make their products.
    d. It has to do with their overall view of the marketplace.

2. Companies that use a sales-oriented marketing strategy primarily use two types of promotion to communicate with their customers:
    a. Public relations and social media
    b. Advertising and personal selling
    c. Advertising and social media
    d. Sales and event marketing

3. A sales-oriented company is:
    a. internally focussed.
    b. externally focussed.
    c. globally focussed.
    d. customer focussed.

4. Which of the following is not a sales-oriented marketing company assumption?
    a. They focus on selling what the company makes, not what the customer wants.
    b. They pay very little attention to the changing needs of their customers and the marketplace.
    c. They put a higher premium on short-term, one-off sales than long-term customer relationships.
    d. Their marketing message is on consumer brand benefits to consumer.

Apply...

1. You are a marketing manager for a large furniture retailer like The Brick or Leon's. You have been asked by your Director to create a 30-second sales-oriented television ad that will help them clear last year's appliance inventory. What would your ad sound like? What would the setting look like? Present your ad to the class.

_____

_____

_____

_____

_____

_____

_____

_____

_____

_____

_____

_____

2. In a paragraph, tell us about a product that you recently purchased as a direct result of a *sales-oriented* pitch by a marketer. What elements of the sales pitch compelled you to purchase the product or service and was your purchase worth it?

_____

_____

_____

_____

_____

_____

_____

_____

_____

_____

_____

_____

The Organization's Focus—Marketing Oriented or Sales Oriented? Marketing Oriented

LO2 Learn how to recognize a marketing-oriented marketing strategy, including what types of goods and services are typically sold using this strategy and what promotional techniques go along with it

A **marketing-oriented company** is externally focused on the consumer's wants and needs and researches the market heavily before releasing a product or service to new and existing consumers. These companies are relationship based and look for ways to continuously add value for consumers by following-up and asking them questions on how to better their offers.

There are three main identifying characteristics of marketing-oriented companies.

- First, *they find out what the market wants* by asking customers for their opinion.

  ◊ Marketing-oriented companies invest in research and survey their existing and potential customers for opinions on what they desire.

- Second, *they respond to market feedback* by providing customers with products and services that are comparable and even better than the former.

  ◊ Apple is a prime example of a company that understands what will excite its customers, and has introduced (up until now) 7 versions of its iPhone product to consumers. Each version is more sophisticated, stylish, and more customer friendly than its predecessor.

- Third, *they create excitement and build anticipation* for their products and services. When customers are thrilled with the performance and value of one product, they'll be more excited for the next release.

  ◊ We've all seen the lineups outside Apple retail locations of people waiting for days in anticipation of a new iPhone or iPad. Disney also creates this type of excitement when releasing many of its films. A $50 million marketing investment on their franchises like Star Wars has grossed billions for the studio. More important, loyal Star Wars fans wait for days in line to see the newest releases, some even dressed in outfit (Table 3.1).

Marketing-oriented companies such as Westjet, Apple, and Porter understand the importance of marketing in creating a well-known brand and look to solve the needs of their customers with an idea, product, or service enhancement. They inquire about customer needs. They ask what customers want and most important, they try to learn how they can *create value for their customers*.

TABLE 3.1 Star Wars movie sales—not bad for a $50 million investment

Star wars movie	Domestic box office sales	Worldwide box office sales
A New Hope	$460,998,007	$786,598,007
The Empire Strikes Back	$290,271,960	$534,171,960
Return of the Jedi	$309,205,079	$572,705,079
The Phantom Menace	$474,544,677	$1,027,044,677
Attack of the Clones	$310,676,740	$656,695,615
Revenge of the Sith	$380,270,577	$848,998,877
The Clone Wars	$35,161,554	$68,695,443
The Force Awakens	$936,662,225	$2,058,662,225
Rogue One: A Star Wars Story	$532,177,324	$1,050,988,488

Source: The numbers, http://www.the-numbers.com/movies/franchise/Star-Wars.

 # Practice...

1. What is the main difference between a sales-oriented company and a marketing-oriented company?
   a. One gives away product while the other company makes the customer pay.
   b. It is the amount of money invested in the company.
   c. It has to do with how they make their products.
   d. It has to do with their overall view of the marketplace.

2. A marketing-oriented company is:
   a. internally focussed.
   b. externally focussed.
   c. globally focussed.
   d. sales focussed.

3. Which of the following is not a marketing-oriented marketing company assumption?
   a. They find out what the customer wants.
   b. They pay very little attention to the changing needs of their customers and the marketplace.
   c. They respond to customer feedback.
   d. Their build excitement and anticipation for their products.

4. To a marketing-oriented company,
   a. focussing on price is the marketer's main concern.
   b. focussing on revenue is the marketer's main concern.
   c. focussing on the brand's development is the marketer's main concern.
   d. focussing on the selling more of the product is the marketer's main concern.

5. At the end of the day, marketing-oriented companies are all about:
   a. creating value for their customers.
   b. creating revenue for the organization.
   c. generating high sales which lead to greater company revenue.
   d. promoting the product internally.

6. An example of a company that would be more sales and not so marketing-oriented is:
   a. Starbucks.
   b. Loblaws.
   c. Zurich Insurance.
   d. WestJet.

 # Apply...

1. You are a marketing manager for WestJet airlines. You have been asked by your Director to create a 30-second marketing-oriented television ad that will tell customers that they will never be bumped off their WestJet seats. What would your ad sound like? What would the setting look like? Present your ad to the class.

_____
_____
_____
_____
_____
_____
_____
_____
_____
_____
_____
_____
_____
_____
_____
_____
_____
_____
_____
_____
_____
_____
_____
_____
_____
_____
_____
_____
_____

to be continued

 **Apply...**

continued

2. In a paragraph, tell us about a product that you recently purchased as a direct result of a marketing-oriented pitch by a marketer. What elements of the marketing pitch compelled you to purchase the product or service and was your purchase worth it?

_____

_____

_____

_____

_____

_____

_____

_____

_____

_____

_____

_____

_____

_____

_____

_____

_____

_____

_____

_____

_____

_____

_____

_____

_____

_____

_____

_____

_____

Creating Value for Customers

L03 Define and understand the types of customer value

Good marketers aim to create products and services that are perceived to have a significant value for their customers. This value keeps customers satisfied and coming back for more.

Nike seems to understand all too well the need to develop strong **customer value** and has tried to attach celebrity and sports endorsers to many of their products. One example is the endorsement of now-retired professional NBA player Michael Jordan and their creation of the Air Jordan basketball shoes. With commercials of Michael Jordan flying through the air and doing the unthinkable, who could resist not wanting to "be like Mike"?

Air Jordans are released every year in a limited edition, with a set amount available. These shoes go for more than $1,000 on social media networks and many sneaker collection websites. Do Air Jordans really make you become a better basketball player? Do they actually help you jump higher, dunk a basketball, and do the impossible? Are they better than Adidas, Converse, or even other Nike basketball shoes? And if they are better, are they worth their value and the much higher price? It's all a matter of how much value one places on the shoes and the perceived benefit they will receive. For many basketball players and sneaker collectors, the answer is—yes, Air Jordans are worth it.

Source: Panatphong/Shutterstock.

In 2015, Nike released the limited edition Air Jordan 1 Pinnacle shoe, featuring 24K Gold plating, a special edition dust-bag packaging, and a scale-textured Air Jordan shoe box. The retail price tag was set at an initial price offering of $400 USD retail at select stores. To loyal Air Jordan customers, this could be perceived as a not only a great deal but great value.

Customer value (Woodruff, 1997) is defined as:

> *a customer perceived preference for and evaluation of those products attributes, attribute performances, and consequences arising from use that facilitate (or block) achieving the customer's goals and purposes in use situations.*

The definition suggests that there are two aspects to customer value: *desired value* and *perceived value*.

- **Desired value** refers to *what customers desire in a product or service*.

- **Perceived value** is the *benefit that a customer believes he or she received from a product after it is purchased*.

Customer-perceived value (Armstrong et al., 2017) is defined as:

> *the customer's evaluation of the difference between all the benefits and all the costs of a marketing offer relative to those of competing offers.*

Customers often do not judge values and costs accurately or objectively, rather they act based upon their *perceived* value of the product. In the case of the Air Jordans, loyalists of the shoe are willing to pay a higher price in order to attain it because they *perceive* the product to have more benefits like dunking a basketball or hitting a clutch three-pointer, than other competing basketball shoe brands.

Customer value does not imply that a product or service has to be of high or better quality. Good customer value means that a customer must be getting a product at a level of quality that they expect with a price that they are happy to pay.

Therefore, customer value can be applied to any product from a watch to a cup of coffee.

For example, if a customer is just looking for *or desires* something to tell time with, then he or she can resort to a more affordable and capable Timex watch. If the customer is looking for a watch that not only tells time but will turn heads at a regatta or the VIP Box at the Kentucky Derby, then he or she might purchase a Rolex brand watch. Both products are reliable and can tell the time but the perceived value that a customer receives from each brand is different. In the case of the cup of coffee, the value of a cup of coffee enjoyed with a friend at a coffee shop might be greater than the value of a cup of coffee made for pennies at home. While the monetary cost of the cup of coffee in both cases might be the same, the value and experience the customer extracts is different.

Practice...

1. What is customer value?
   a. When an individual becomes attached to a marketing campaign.
   b. The relationship between benefits and the sacrifice necessary to obtain those benefits.
   c. The relationship between goods and services.
   d. When expensive products deliver satisfaction.

2. Enjoying a $25 glass of wine with a friend at an upscale Michelin-rated restaurant versus at home is a:
   a. desired value.
   b. perceived value.
   c. perspective value.
   d. customer value.

3. Creating a valuable customer experience should be the focus of:
   a. all companies.
   b. a sales-oriented company.
   c. a marketing-oriented company.
   d. larger and more popular branded companies.

4. John needs a "good old-fashioned" tennis shoe to play in a tournament this weekend but is not into brands and does not want to pay a lot of money on the shoe. The value he places on the tennis shoe is a _____ value.
   a. desired
   b. perceived
   c. perspective
   d. customer

5. Good customer value means that a customer:
   a. values the brand, product, or service of a company.
   b. is getting a bargain on one of their favourite products.
   c. must be getting a product at a level of quality that they expect, with a price that they are happy to pay.
   d. is not willing to pay more for a product that is of superior quality.

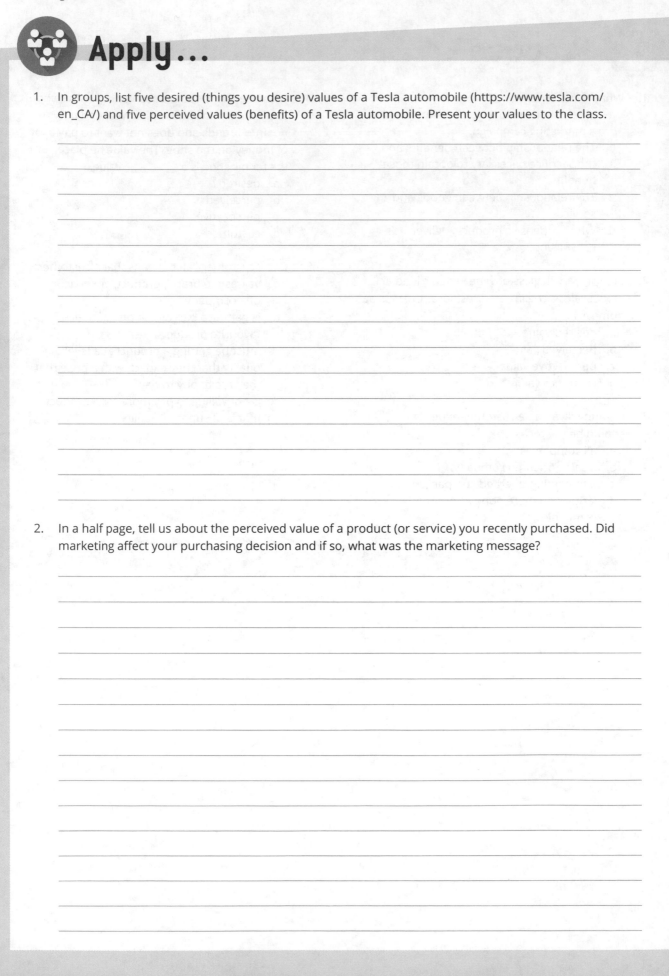

Apply...

1. In groups, list five desired (things you desire) values of a Tesla automobile (https://www.tesla.com/en_CA/) and five perceived values (benefits) of a Tesla automobile. Present your values to the class.

2. In a half page, tell us about the perceived value of a product (or service) you recently purchased. Did marketing affect your purchasing decision and if so, what was the marketing message?

Strong Customer Satisfaction Leads to Strong Customer Relationships

LO4 Understand how customer satisfaction leads to stronger customer relationships

Marketers of established brands work hard to attract and retain customers by offering them products that have high *perceived value*. Their marketing efforts reinforce this value and are premised via a *value proposition* which aims to convince and reinforce to customers that their product or service will add more value or better solve a problem than other competitors in the category.

The end result of an effective marketing orientation strategy is customer satisfaction and loyalty.

Customer satisfaction is defined as . . .

> the extent to which a product's perceived performance matches a
> buyer's expectation. (Armstrong et al., 2017)

Customer satisfaction is a term used frequently in marketing to measure how products and services supplied by a company meet or surpass the customer's expectations. When the product or service does NOT reach consumers' expectations, the result is *dissatisfaction* and a potential customer loss. Customer dissatisfaction can also cause brands to step up their service to deliver a higher perceived value experience for their customers.

The Table 3.2 indicates the satisfaction levels of cellular phone brands across the United States.

TABLE 3.2 Satisfaction levels of cellular phone brands in the United States

Smartphone Customer Satisfaction—May 23, 2017		
Model	**Manufacturer**	**ACSI Score (0–100 Scale)**
iPhone SE	Apple	87
Galaxy S6 edge+	Samsung	86
iPhone 7 Plus	Apple	86
Galaxy S6 edge	Samsung	85
Galaxy S7	Samsung	84
Galaxy S7 edge	Samsung	84
iPhone 6 Plus	Apple	83
iPhone 6s Plus	Apple	83
iPhone 7	Apple	83
Galaxy Note 5	Samsung	82
Galaxy Note 4	Samsung	81
Galaxy S5	Samsung	80
iPhone 5	Apple	80
iPhone 5s	Apple	80
iPhone 6s	Apple	80

Galaxy S6	Samsung	79
iPhone 6	Apple	79
Galaxy J3	Samsung	77
Galaxy S4	Samsung	76
Galaxy Grand Prime	Samsung	75
Moto G	Motorola	75
LG G4	LG	73
Galaxy Core Prime	Samsung	70

Source: Used by permission from: Benchmarks by Smartphone Brand: Retrieved From: www.theacsi. org/customer-satisfaction-benchmarks/benchmarks-by-brand/benchmarks-for-smartphones.

Though customer satisfaction scores are high in comparison to other product categories, newer model smart phones with more "bells and whistles" and the latest technological innovations, score higher than older model mobile phones.

The American Customer Satisfaction Index (ACSI) is a customer satisfaction index for products and services used by many companies to assess whether their products or services are meeting and/or exceeding customers' expectations. By looking at the variables *of customer expectations, perceived quality, perceived value, customer satisfaction, and customer complaints*, marketers can assess how satisfied and ultimately how loyal a customer is to a brand or company (Figure 1).

It is the aim of all marketers to develop a *strong relationship* with customers that have high customer satisfaction scores with their brands.

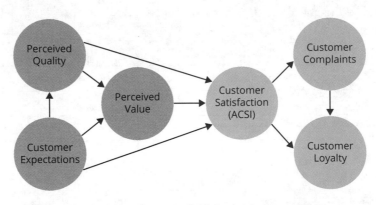

FIGURE 1 The American Customer Satisfaction Index model.

Source: Used by permission from: "American Customer Satisfaction Index Model" in American Index, Retrieved from: www.theacsi.org/about-acsi/ the-science-of-customer-satisfaction.

Practice...

1. Customer satisfaction is:
   a. when a customer sells an item online for a lower price than they bought it for.
   b. when customers feel they are getting a lot of value.
   c. the end result of an effective marketing orientation and occurs when the good or service has met the customer's needs and expectations.
   d. when a customer purchases an item but is not happy about their purchase.

2. A customer value proposition aims to:
   a. convince and reinforce to customers that their product or service will add more value or better solve a problem than the competition.
   b. differentiate between desired and perceived value.
   c. address the amount of revenue a company proposes to generate as a result of the marketing campaign.
   d. convince and reinforce to customers that from a value perspective, their product or service choice will be just the same as the competition's offer.

3. When the product or service does NOT reach consumers' expectations, the result is:
   a. dissatisfaction.
   b. a less valuable product.
   c. a shift in strategy by the marketer.
   d. increased customer satisfaction.

4. The American Customer Satisfaction Index (ACSI) is a customer satisfaction index that is used by companies to assess:
   a. the satisfaction of their brands.
   b. the dissatisfaction of their brands.
   c. whether a company's products are meeting or exceeding customers' expectations.
   d. whether a company's products or services are satisfying the internal needs of the organization.

5. The ACSI assesses and measures:
   a. the revenue generated by products and services.
   b. customer acquisition, customer retention, customer attrition, and customer trial.
   c. customer expectations, perceived quality, perceived value, customer satisfaction, customer complaints, and customer loyalty.
   d. how many customers agree with company's value proposition.

 **Apply...**

1. Individual Activity:

   Using the ACSI rate, how satisfied you are with your mobile service provider. Use a scale of 0–5 (0 being the lowest and 5 being the highest score) to grade your customer expectations, perceived quality, perceived value, customer satisfaction, and customer complaints. Present your scores to the class. Your scale would look like this:

Cell Phone—Satisfaction Survey					
	Very satisfied	**Somewhat satisfied**	**Neutral**	**Somewhat dissatisfied**	**Very dissatisfied**
Customer Expectations	5	4	3	2	1
Perceived Quality	5	4	3	2	1
Perceived Value	5	4	3	2	1
Customer Satisfaction	5	4	3	2	1
Customer Complaints	5	4	3	2	1

What did you think about this survey? What did you like about it? What didn't you like about it?

_____

_____

_____

_____

_____

_____

_____

_____

_____

_____

_____

_____

_____

_____

_____

_____

to be continued

Apply...

continued

2. Group Activity:

   The definition of **value proposition** is "which aims to convince and reinforce to customers that their product or service will add more value or better solve a problem than other competitors in the category".

   Reflecting upon the Air Jordan shoes discuss in this chapter, pretend your team is the marketing agency for Nike and your task is to create a value proposition for the latest Nike Basketball shoe (you will have to go online to find the newest releases) being released by Nike. What will your value proposition look like?

Relationship Marketing

LO5 Learn what relationship marketing is as well as look at some related strategies

Think about brands like Cineplex, Canada Goose, Mountain Equipment Co-op (MEC), Tim Horton's, Loblaws, WestJet, and Pizza Pizza. They are examples of Canadian companies that provide exceptional value and experiences for their customers. Their secret for success is not only in their marketing-oriented strategy but their ability to form a relationship or bond with their customers that goes beyond the point of purchase.

Relationship Marketing is defined as (American Marketing Association):

> *Marketing with the conscious aim to develop and manage long-term and/or trusting relationships with customers, distributors, suppliers, or other parties in the marketing environment.*

A company with a relationship marketing focus tries to build rapport and a more long-term, "two-way" relationship with their customers. They continuously enquire about their customer's needs and wants and offer products and services that are relative and of customer value.

The benefits of relationship marketing include increased word-of-mouth, repeat business, and a willingness on the customer's part to provide valuable feedback to the company. This has been facilitated with the growth of more collaborative and social communication channels such as the internet, social media and text, and mobile platforms.

Payne and Ballantyne's **Six Market Model**, identifies six markets which they claim are central to relationship marketing. Their model argues that if marketing is to be effective, it has to develop relationships with not only the *final customer* market but the *referral, supplier, influencer, recruitment, and internal markets as well.*

Customer markets include wholesalers, middlemen such as retail stores, and new or existing final customers of the product.

Referral marketing is developing and implementing a marketing plan that focuses on having a trustworthy source to advocate for your product or service to consumers. These advocates can include family and community members.

Supplier markets aims to build relationships with people and organizations that provide physical and knowledge-based resources to your business. Developing solid relationships with this market will help you provide great value to your customers, which is conflict-free and cost-effective.

Influencer markets consist of people and organizations that can influence your business and your customer's business. Examples include investors, unions, regulators, news media, evaluators (such as *Consumer Reports*), environmental groups, political and government agencies, and even your competitors. A good public relations and media-relations campaigns will help you to get these groups on your side.

Recruitment markets include potential employees and related third-party staffing agencies. Employees are often very effective advocates and have a natural incentive to see your business succeed. Here, you will try to select employees best suited to provide your customers with excellent service and products.

Internal markets include actual employees. This market is very important for two reasons. First, as already mentioned, employees can be strong advocates and marketing ambassadors for your company. Secondly, they represent the brand and are the face of the company that is presented to your customers. How they interact and treat customers will have a strong influence on building long-term customer relationships. Companies that have placed

FIGURE 2 The six markets model.

Source: Based on Payne, C. & Ballantyne, D. (1991). Relationship marketing: Bringing quality customer service and marketing together, Butterworth-Heinemann, p. 264.

a premium on employee selection, training, and customer service will most likely see customers that keep coming back for more, if they have a positive customer focused experience (Figure 2).

Companies that utilize the six model strategy effectively include financial services companies specifically The Big 5 Canadian banks leverage their large customer, employee, and supplier base to build strong relationships with customers and promote products and services.

Practice...

1. Which of the following best describes relationship marketing?
   a. When relationships are used for promotion.
   b. A strategy that is used to only increase sales for a business.
   c. When customers befriend each other and communicate about a product.
   d. A strategy that focuses on keeping and improving relationships with current customers.

2. Payne and Ballantyne identify _____ markets which they claim are central to relationship marketing.
   a. three
   b. six
   c. nine
   d. twelve

3. A company with a relationship marketing focus tries to build a long-term, _____ relationship with their customers.
   a. one-way
   b. two-way
   c. three-way
   d. four-way

4. The market that aims to build relationships with people and organizations that provide physical and knowledge-based resources to your business is the:
   a. customer market.
   b. referral market.
   c. supplier market.
   d. influencer market.

5. The market that may include investors, unions, regulators, the news media, and evaluators is the:
   a. customer market.
   b. referral market.
   c. supplier market.
   d. influencer market.

Apply…

1. Canadian Tire has gone to considerable lengths to enhance the relationship they have with their market segments in Canada. What are some of the things they have done? Search out some their strategies via their website (http://www.canadiantire.ca/en.html) or by doing a search online regarding their marketing strategy initiatives over the past several years.

    _____

    _____

    _____

    _____

    _____

    _____

    _____

    _____

    _____

    _____

    _____

    _____

    _____

2. Explain how word of mouth (WOM) marketing impacts businesses. What impact (positive or negative) does WOM have via social media platforms? Explain your reasoning with an example or two.

    _____

    _____

    _____

    _____

    _____

    _____

    _____

    _____

    _____

    _____

    _____

    _____

    _____

    _____

    _____

    _____

KNOW...

Learning Objectives

1. A sales-oriented marketing strategy is one in which a company focuses all of their marketing efforts on selling the product that they produce. Companies that use a sales-oriented marketing strategy are so focused on selling their products that they are often blindsided by changing customer needs and technological advances.

2. Marketing-oriented companies are businesses that actively seek ways to understand what their customers want and create products specifically designed for those customers. Ensuring there is a demand for their products and services is one of the most vital elements of a marketing-oriented company. The main differences between a sales-oriented company and a marketing-oriented company have to do with their overall view of the marketplace. A sales-oriented company is very internally focused and looks to sell products that the company is successful at making. A marketing-oriented firm is externally focused on the consumer's wants and needs.

3. Customer value does not imply that a product or service has to be of high or better quality. Good customer value means that a customer must be getting a product at a level of quality that they expect with a price that they are happy to pay. There are two aspects to customer value: *desired value* and *perceived value.* It is important for marketers to recognize the type of value that the customer is seeking when selecting a product or service.

4. Customer satisfaction is a term used frequently in marketing to measure how products and services supplied by a company meet or surpass the customer's expectations.

5. Relationship marketing is a strategy that focuses on keeping and improving relationships with current customers. A company with a relationship marketing focus tries to build rapport and a more long-term, "two-way" relationship with their customers. The Six Market Model states that if marketing is to be effective, it has to develop relationships with not only the final customer market but the *referral, supplier, influencer, recruitment, and internal markets as well.*

Key Terms

Customer-Perceived Value: "The customer's evaluation of the difference between all the benefits and all the costs of a marketing offer relative to those of competing offers."

Customer Satisfaction: "The extent to which a product's perceived performance matches a buyer's expectation."

Customer Value: "A customer perceived preference for and evaluation of those products attributes, attribute performances, and consequences arising from use that facilitate (or block) achieving the customer's goals and purposes in use situations."

Desired Value: What customers desire in a product or service.

Marketing-Oriented Company: Externally focused on the consumer's wants and needs and researches the market heavily before releasing a product or service to new and existing consumers.

Perceived Value: The benefit that a customer believes he or she received from a product after it is purchased.

Relationship Marketing: "Marketing with the conscious aim to develop and manage long-term and/or trusting relationships with customers, distributors, suppliers, or other parties in the marketing environment."

Sales-Oriented Company: Very internally focused and looks to sell products to the market that they are successful at making.

Six Market Model: Six markets—customer, referral, supplier, influencer, recruitment, and internal which should be looked at by marketers in order to build their brand.

The American Customer Satisfaction Index (ACSI): A customer satisfaction index for products and services which looks at the variables of customer expectations, perceived quality, perceived value, customer satisfaction, and Customer Complaints, to assess how satisfied and ultimately how loyal a customer is to a brand or company.

Value Proposition: A statement which aims to convince and reinforce to customers that their product or service will add more value or better solve a problem than other competitors in the category. The end result of an effective marketing orientation strategy is customer satisfaction and loyalty.

Answers to Practice

The Organization's Focus—Marketing Oriented or Sales Oriented? Sales Oriented

1. d   2. b   3. a   4. d

The Organization's Focus—Marketing Oriented or Sales Oriented? Sales Oriented

1. d   2. b   3. b   4. c   5. a   6. c

Creating Value for Customers

1. b   2. b   3. a   4. a   5. c

Strong Customer Satisfaction Leads to Strong Customer Relationships

1. c   2. a   3. a   4. c   5. c

Relationship Marketing

1. d   2. b   3. b   4. c   5. d

References

American Marketing Association's Online Marketing Dictionary.

Armstrong, Gary, Kotler, Philip, Marketing: An Introduction, 13th Ed., ©2017. Reprinted and Electronically reproduced by permission of Pearson Education, Inc., New York, NY.

Armstrong, Kotler, Trifts, Buchwitz. (2017). *Marketing, An Introduction*. Pearson Canada; 2017.

Hacket R. Disney's 'Star Wars' practically markets itself. Retrieved from http://fortune.com/2015/12/08/star-wars-marketing.

Payne, C. & Ballantyne, D. (1991). Relationship Marketing. Bringing Quality Customer Service and Marketing Together, Butterworth-Heinemann, p. 264.

The Numbers, http://www.the-numbers.com/movies/franchise/Star-Wars.

Woodruff, Robert B, Customer Value: The next source for competitive advantage, Journal of the Academic Marketing Science., March 1997, 25: 139.

4 Consumer Behaviour in Marketing

LEARNING OBJECTIVES

LO1 Define consumer behaviour

LO2 Understand why consumer behaviour is important to marketers

LO3 Identify the factors that affect consumer behaviour

LO4 Identify some of the models used to explain consumer purchasing behaviour

LO5 Explain some of the ways marketers study consumer insights and behaviour

LEARN...

As we know, without consumers most—if not all—business would not survive. Since businesses cannot live without consumers, it is important for them to understand how consumers behave relative to the products and services businesses offer or are preparing to offer.

We also know that today's consumers have more choice and options than ever, with multiple companies competing for their attention, time, and money. Marketers who monitor consumer behaviour are able to develop strategies and product solutions that differentiate them from the competitive pack, as well as appeal specifically to their customers. In the long run, this helps to build their brand and provides them with greater market share.

The study of consumer behaviour is interested in every aspect of a consumer's interaction with a product and, in particular, the psychological, personal, cultural, and social factors that cause a consumer to choose one product over the other. The study of consumer behaviour asks questions like:

- Who buys a product and/or service?
- What products do consumers seek, purchase, and use?
- Why do they buy it?
- Where do they buy it?
- How do they interact with the product and/or service?
- How loyal are they to the product and/or service?
- How do they dispose of the product and/or service?

Insight into these factors provides marketers with an opportunity to dissect and study existing and prospective consumers at a micro level and to answer some key behavioural purchasing questions. These insights allow marketers the opportunity to:

- better develop products and services that are attractive and useful to consumers;

- improve their chance for brand survival and prosperity;
- differentiate their brand from the competition;
- identify opportunities that are not currently met; and
- create strategies, products, and services that effectively target consumers.

What Is Consumer Behaviour?

L01 Define consumer behaviour

Marketing is more than just memorable taglines, catchy phrases, and jingles. In fact, the most memorable campaigns were created as a direct result of good marketers doing their homework and understanding their consumers' wants and why they do what they do.

- Why do you bank with a credit union when you could be banking with one of the Big 5 bank brands?
- Why does your best friend prefer Android products over Apple?
- Why are you willing to spend more on lululemon athletic wear when the Fabletics brand is 50% cheaper and delivers to your door?
- Why does your partner prefer Colgate and you prefer Crest?

Most of the time, the answers to these questions aren't obvious. But to marketers, these questions affect the product development, pricing, distribution, and promotion strategies that they will develop and offer consumers. It is important for the marketer to understand how consumers make purchasing decisions and the factors and interactions that influence them to purchase their favourite products and services.

According to Kotler and Keller (2011),

> *Consumer buying behaviour is the study of the ways of buying and disposing of goods, services, ideas or experiences by the individuals, groups and organizations in order to satisfy their needs and wants.*

To Kotler and Keller, understanding **consumer buying behaviour** provides marketers with an insight into how consumers will respond to a new product or service and why they make the choices and decisions that they make. Understanding consumer behaviour further allows marketers the chance to identify opportunities that are not currently met in the market by other brands and to effectively develop and differentiate strategies that reflect the specific needs and wants of their audience.

Consumer behaviour is in essence the psychology of marketing and it seeks to explore and find out why consumers *make the decisions that they make, do what they do, and buy what they buy.* Marketers and those that study consumer behaviour realize that studying the behaviour of consumers is an ongoing process and a journey that is inspired long before a consumer purchases a product and continues even after the product is consumed by the customer.

Besides psychology and marketing, other related disciplines to consumer behaviour include economics, anthropology, and sociology (Figure 1).

FIGURE 1 Consumer behaviour and closely related disciplines.

 # Practice...

1. Why is the study of consumer behaviour not important to marketers?
   a. It provides them with insights into how consumers will respond to a new product or service.
   b. It helps to steer the direction for pricing strategies.
   c. It identifies opportunities in the market that may have gone unnoticed.
   d. It provides insights into how competitors will respond to your product or service.

2. Consumer buying behaviour won't provide marketers with insights on:
   a. how consumers voted.
   b. how consumers will respond to a new product or service.
   c. what mobile devices are most popular.
   d. the products that are being developed by competitors.

3. Consumer behaviour should not:
   a. involve all levels of the organization.
   b. cease once the marketer has achieved 100% market share.
   c. be an ongoing process.
   d. keep an eye on what customers are thinking and doing

4. Marketers can develop a more effective marketing campaign once:
   a. they understand the behaviour of their consumers.
   b. they set marketing objectives.
   c. they set marketing strategies.
   d. they set marketing tactics.

5. Consumer behaviour should:
   a. involve all levels of the organization.
   b. not look for opportunities in the market.
   c. always consider the budget a company has to spend on a marketing campaign.
   d. only focus on a small portion of the population because of the costs that are involved.

 **Apply...**

1. Individually, reflect upon something you have purchased in the past year or eighteen that replaced a product or service you were using. How is the new purchase meeting needs which were previously not being met?

_____

_____

_____

_____

_____

_____

_____

_____

_____

_____

_____

_____

_____

2. In groups, make a list of things that influence your purchase behaviour. Why do these things impact your purchase decision? Be ready to share your results with the class.

_____

_____

_____

_____

_____

_____

_____

_____

_____

_____

_____

_____

_____

_____

_____

_____

Why Is Consumer Behaviour Important for Marketers?

L02 Understand why consumer behaviour is important to marketers

In 2017, Retail POS software manufacturer Vend noticed that consumers don't want to waste their precious time wandering around the endless aisles of enormous stores, but want ease and efficiency in the form of smaller stores with specialized selections. This may explain why retail giants like Target, Best Buy, Ikea, and even Tim Hortons are investing more today in smaller-format stores to accommodate a consumer desire for more curated selections (Vend, 2017).

On a daily basis, consumers face a myriad of choices. Their opinions, needs, and wants change, and they are constantly bombarded with information, products, and services that are better, stronger, and faster than the ones they are currently using.

They are seeking solutions from the brands that they know and trust, and this requires marketing departments not only to keep an eye on consumer shifts but to create strategies that resonate with consumers and differentiate their brand.

Knowing what the shifts and trends in consumer behaviour are will help an organization to better understand opportunities that are not currently met in the market and to tweak existing product and service offerings. A more careful analysis helps to produce a more exact prediction about the behaviour of consumers in relation to a product or service. Overall, marketers need to study the behaviour of consumers so that they may be better able to (Babin, 2009):

- Build their business and strategy
- Assess the products people buy
- Assess why they buy them
- Assess the attributes they seek in their products
- Decide what business orientation to take on:

  ◊ Differentiated

  ◊ Undifferentiated

  ◊ Niche

A recent example of a change in consumer behaviour is clearly visible in the eating habits of younger Gen Z consumers—those born in the mid-1990s onward and are now in the 5 to 20-year-old category. Gen Z (the generation following Millenials) really think cooking is cool. They are more likely to eat fresh home-cooked meals and, when they dine out, prefer to eat healthier at Quick Service restaurants (QSRs). They prefer stove-top to microwave cooking and are more intuitive cooks. They are the most ethnically diverse generation, so to them ethnic foods are the norm. This strong generation of 68 million people are financially cautious and demand good value from the foods they consume, both in and out of home. They hate corporate greed, don't trust brands, and demand transparency. Also, Because Generation Z uses technology so customarily, they are more likely to make well-researched and informed purchase decisions (Yohn, 2013).

Restaurateurs like McDonald's are monitoring and responding to this shift in the values and eating patterns of Gen Z and have added combinations with a more ethnic influence to their menus. McTaster Sandwiches like the Mexican Chipotle Burger and the Thai Sweet Chili Chicken, along with salads like the

Grilled Greek Chicken Salad, are all new offerings by the restaurateur to address shifts in consumer tastes and appetites. McDonald's now practices greater transparency and provides more menu and caloric information in order to satisfy this information-dependent generation.

Practice...

1. It is important for marketers to study consumer behaviour because:
   a. it allows them to understand the factors that influence the buying decision.
   b. it sets corporate policy.
   c. it affects the direction of the corporation.
   d. it will set the tone for corporate functions and events.

2. Deciding what factors influence the purchasing decision is the premise behind:
   a. marketing.
   b. social psychology.
   c. economics.
   d. consumer behaviour.

3. Consumer behaviour is important to marketers when it comes to:
   a. setting the best customer price on a product or service.
   b. deciding where to promote a product or service.
   c. deciding when to launch a product or service.
   d. planning and assessing their distribution and merchandising partnerships.

4. Finding out the best method of consumer promotion that will attract customers to buy a product is usually the responsibility of:
   a. the accounting department.
   b. the HR department.
   c. the marketing department.
   d. the whole organization.

5. After reading the results of a customer survey, a major supermarket found out that candy purchases are made at the beginning of a shopping trip. As a result, they decided to place their generic candy brands at the front of the supermarket. This was most likely done because:
   a. of a shift in consumer buying patterns.
   b. a decline in sales.
   c. a decline in customer traffic.
   d. more competing brands fighting for shelf space.

 **Apply…**

1. Pizza Pizza is looking to introduce a new item to its menu that it hopes will attract the emerging Asian and South East Asian Canadian communities. Design a three-item pizza menu that is reflective of these two communities. Here is some information about the demographic:

    https://tinyurl.com/flextext-asian-community and

    https://tinyurl.com/flextext-eating-patterns.

    _____

    _____

    _____

    _____

    _____

    _____

    _____

    _____

    _____

    _____

    _____

    _____

2. Nike is looking to boost the awareness of its brand among Gen Z consumers. What media would you use to communicate your message and what would you as a marketer do to capture the awareness and interest of this key demographic, and why?

    _____

    _____

    _____

    _____

    _____

    _____

    _____

    _____

    _____

    _____

    _____

What Affects Consumer Behaviour?

LO3 Identify the factors that affect consumer behaviour

Consumer buying behaviour includes numerous factors believed to have some level of effect on the purchasing decisions made by customers. Though marketers cannot control these factors and may find it difficult to identify the exact reasons why a consumer purchases and prefers one product or service over another one, these factors may be able to shed some light on a consumer's purchasing decision and must be taken into account.

Cultural Factors

Cultural factors exert a broad and deep influence on consumer behaviour, and marketers need to understand the role played by the buyer's culture and subculture.

Every member of society has a culture, and marketers need to be cognizant of the cultural shifts and influences on the buying behaviour of consumers across groups. Therefore, marketers must adjust to these variations in order to prevent embarrassing cultural blunders.

Each culture contains subcultures, or groups of people with shared value systems based on common life experiences or situations. Subcultures can include nationalities, religions, racial groups, and geographic regions. Often, a single subculture can make up a market segment that marketers aim at by tailoring a product to the subculture's needs. For example, celiac disease has dramatically increased the demand for gluten-free (GF) products and has created a huge industry. Companies that better monitored the change in eating patterns of consumers and created GF products were able to fill a void in the marketplace and position themselves as category leaders, innovators, and even influencers in this category.

Psychological Factors

In daily life, consumers are affected by many issues that are *unique to their thought processes*. **Psychological factors** can include perception of a need or situation, a person's ability to learn or understand information, and an individual's attitude. Each person will respond to a marketing message based on his or her perceptions and attitudes. Therefore, marketers must take these psychological factors into account when creating campaigns, ensuring that a specific campaign will appeal to its target audience.

Personal Factors

Personal factors are characteristics that are *specific to a person* and may not relate to other people within the same group. These characteristics may include how a person makes decisions, their unique habits and interests, and opinions. When considering personal factors, decisions are also influenced by age, gender, background, culture, and other personal issues.

For example, an older person will likely exhibit different consumer behaviours than a younger person, meaning that they will choose products differently and spend their money on items that may not interest a younger person.

Social Factors

The fourth factor that has a significant impact on consumer behaviour is the **social factor**. Social factors greatly *influence* how people respond to marketing messages and make purchasing decisions.

A person can be influenced by family, work or school clubs, or any group of people that he/she affiliates with or looks up to. It can also include a person's social class, which involves income, living conditions, and level of education.

A person's social class can also influence a consumer's response to marketing messages. People of similar social classes (that is, income, living conditions, and level of education) tend to act, respond, and purchase in a similar manner. Marketers can effectively predict the purchasing behaviour of consumers by looking at the history similar social class members and then target a campaign to new and/or aspiring customers.

Practice...

1. When Reebok wanted to test a new running shoe, they gave samples to college freshman students throughout the country and asked for feedback. Reebok was using which of the following factors to influence consumers?
   a. Cultural
   b. Social
   c. Psychological
   d. Personal

2. A person's age is a _____that may affect the buyer's purchasing decision.
   a. cultural factor
   b. psychological factor
   c. personal factor
   d. social factor

3. Belonging to a hunting and fishing club is a _____that may affect the buyer's purchasing decision.
   a. cultural factor
   b. psychological factor
   c. personal factor
   d. social factor

4. A person's attitude toward a political candidate or party is a _____that may affect an individual's voting decision.
   a. cultural factor
   b. psychological factor
   c. personal factor
   d. social factor

5. When Gatorade wanted to test a new energy drink flavour with a price tag of $8 per bottle, they gave samples to gym members at exclusive and upscale gyms across the country and asked for feedback. Gatorade was using _____factors to influence consumers.
   a. cultural
   b. psychological
   c. personal
   d. social

 Apply...

1. Fitbit is looking to introduce protein and energy bars to the market. Which of the four consumer behaviour factors (cultural, psychological, social, or personal) would you use to best reach out to consumers, and why?

_____

_____

_____

_____

_____

_____

_____

_____

_____

_____

_____

_____

_____

_____

2. Gatorade is introducing a new energy drink flavour. What personal and/or psychological factors would you use to sell this new product to (1) teens 16–19, (2) adults 24–34, and (3) adults 45–54, and why?

_____

_____

_____

_____

_____

_____

_____

_____

_____

_____

_____

_____

_____

_____

Consumer Behaviour Models

LO4 Identify some of the models used to explain consumer purchasing behaviour

Why do individuals buy different goods and services for personal consumption?
Why do certain groups of people prefer different items than other groups?
How did they come up with these decisions to purchase?

The buying behaviour of final consumers is influenced by various factors. Through research and observation, several models have been developed that help to further explain the decision-making process and why consumers make decisions, including the *black box, personal variables, and complex models.*

The black box model, also called the **stimulus-response model**, is one of the simpler consumer behaviour models. The black box can be thought of as the region of the consumer's brain that is responsible for purchasing decisions. Environmental stimuli, such as economics, technology, and culture, combine with marketing stimuli, like the product, price, and promotion, inside the black box, where decisions are made. The outcomes of the thinking that takes place in the black box are the buyer's responses. These refer to buying attitudes, purchase behaviour, and brand preference of a consumer (Figure 2).

Unlike the black box model, where external stimuli are the main focus, the **personal variable model** studies the internal factors that affect consumer behaviour and purchasing decisions. This model specifically ignores external stimuli, such as marketing techniques, and concentrates on internal psychological variables like personal opinions, belief systems, lifestyle, values, traditions, and goals. These variables include lifestyle, motivations, and personality. It also looks at individual decision-making processes, such as problem recognition, alternative evaluation, as well as post-purchase behaviour (Figure 3).

The third consumer behaviour model is the **complex or comprehensive model**. As the name suggests, the complex model considers all the internal and external stimuli when studying purchasing behaviour. It is beneficial because

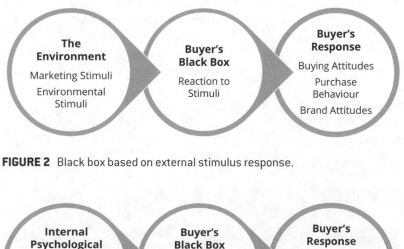

FIGURE 2 Black box based on external stimulus response.

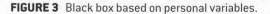

FIGURE 3 Black box based on personal variables.

FIGURE 4 Black box based on the complex or comprehensive variables.

it is the only model that can be used to study how different external stimuli react in different types of personalities and demographics. Because of the large amount of variables required, it is sometimes difficult to determine the accuracy of the conclusions drawn from these complex model studies (Figure 4).

Practice...

1. The stimulus-response model looks at customers' _____ environment when deciding to purchase a product or service.
   a. external
   b. internal
   c. external and internal
   d. peripheral

2. The complex or comprehensive variable model looks at customers' _____ environment when deciding to purchase a product or service.
   a. external
   b. internal
   c. external and internal
   d. peripheral

3. The personal variable model looks at customers' _____ environment when deciding to purchase a product or service.
   a. external
   b. internal
   c. external and internal
   d. peripheral

4. The consumer behaviour model that analyzes a consumer's media consumption and its impact on his or her purchase behaviour is known as the:
   a. stimulus-response model.
   b. personal variable model.
   c. comprehensive or complex model.
   d. social value model.

5. The consumer behaviour model that analyzes a consumer's lifestyle behaviour and its impact on his or her purchase behaviour is known as the:
   a. stimulus-response model.
   b. personal variable model.
   c. comprehensive or complex model.
   d. social value model.

 **Apply...**

1. Activity—Guys do this one!

   Using the black box model (environmental stimuli—economics, technology, and culture, combine with marketing stimuli—product, price, and promotion) provide examples of what would impact an 18–24-year-old male consumer's decision to purchase a used automobile.

   _____

   _____

   _____

   _____

   _____

   _____

   _____

   _____

   _____

   _____

   _____

   _____

   _____

2. Activity—Girls do this one!

   Using the personal variable model (concentrates on internal psychological variables like personal opinions, belief systems, lifestyle, values, traditions, and goals) list some of the internal stimuli that would impact an 18–24-year-old female consumer's decision to rent a downtown condominium.

   _____

   _____

   _____

   _____

   _____

   _____

   _____

   _____

   _____

   _____

   _____

   _____

   _____

   _____

How Is Consumer Behaviour Studied

L05 Explain some of the ways marketers study consumer insights and behaviour

In April 2017, Tim Horton's launched its Perfect Latte kiosk in Toronto. According to the company's president, the kiosk was opened as a response to consumer demand for higher-quality coffee and the need to deliver premium beverages to Canadians in a more comfortable and more mainstream restaurant than a high-end coffee shop (Kolm, 2017).

How did Tim Horton's come up with this differentiating marketing strategy? How did they know where and when to launch their kiosk?

The response to these questions most likely lies in the company's ability to gauge and study the coffee needs and wants of Canadian consumers. How did they go about in accomplishing this?

There are many ways to study consumer behaviour, but the three most common ways include:

1. **Focus Groups**: Getting several consumers together at the same time and place offers a chance to ask marketing questions and determine how consumers feel about existing or new products.

2. **Surveys:** Asking people for input allows the marketing group to understand how consumers feel, what they want, and how they will react. If it is clear that consumers are not happy with a current product or will not want a future product, companies can make accommodations for consumer behaviour and capitalize on greater sales elsewhere.

3. **Track Sales History:** Past consumer behaviour helps to predict future consumer behaviour. By studying what consumers have done historically, companies can make predictions about what customers will do in response to changes. Think about the last time you went to the market and scanned your rewards card. The data collected from your purchases is combined with millions of other transactions to better understand consumer behaviour.

Once companies have a better understanding of consumer buying habits and consumer behaviour, they have valuable information about what consumers want, how they learn about products, and how they spend their money. Marketing takes this information to create ad campaigns about existing and new products with the intention of creating a demand for products and services. By understanding consumer behaviour, the marketing department of a company can effectively create an entire campaign to support the awareness and demand for a product or service.

Practice...

1. Getting several consumers together at the same time and place to gain their perspective on a new product launch from Apple is a:
   a. focus group.
   b. survey.
   c. sales tracking exercise.
   d. mall intercept.

2. Jon received a letter in the mail asking him to offer his opinions on a product he recently purchased from a big box hardware store. He was most likely asked to participate in a:
   a. focus group.
   b. survey.
   c. sales tracking exercise.
   d. mall intercept.

3. Rene has a loyalty card from her favourite bookstore. The loyalty program is a strategy used by the bookstore's marketing department to:
   a. monitor customers' opinions about a new product.
   b. track current and past behaviour and to predict future purchases at the bookstore.
   c. survey the opinions of customers about new book products.
   d. clear unwanted inventory by giving Rene discounts.

4. The decision by an athletic shoe brand to launch an urban tough running shoe at a 24-hour pop-up shop in downtown Montreal, most likely came about as a result of a:
   a. sales tracking exercise.
   b. focus group.
   c. an analysis of the consumer's social environment.
   d. an analysis of the consumer's psychological environment.

5. If you wanted to ask a group of 5,000 people their opinion about a new magazine, you would likely use a(n) _____ to reach and gauge your consumers.
   a. focus group
   b. email survey
   c. sales tracking exercise
   d. mall intercept

1. Come up with five questions that you would ask young adult consumers (18–24 years of age) in a focus group about tide's product called Tide Pods. (https://tide.ca/en-ca)

2. After a lengthy discussion involving a number of focus groups, Canada's Wonderland learned that its primary consumers (teens, 14–18 years of age) only come to the park to enjoy the rides, but don't purchase food or drinks at the confection stands throughout the park. Come up with a marketing campaign to address this information. What media would you use and why? What would your marketing campaign look like?

KNOW...

Learning Objectives

1. Marketers and those that study consumer behaviour realize that studying the behaviour of consumers is an ongoing process and a journey that is inspired long before a consumer purchases a product and continues even after the product is consumed by the customer. Consumer behaviour incorporates the disciplines of psychology, marketing, economics, anthropology, and sociology, to get a better appreciation of the purchasing behaviour of consumers.

2. Everyday new trends and choices are introduced to consumers and, as a result, their opinions, needs, and wants change. Marketers need to stay on top of consumer trends, if they are to deliver the best brand experiences to their consumers.

3. The study of consumer behaviour is interested in every aspect of the consumers' interaction with a product and, in particular, the psychological, personal, cultural, and social factors that cause a consumer to choose one product over the other.

4. Through research and observation, several models have been developed that help to further explain the decision-making process and why consumers make decisions. Three models in particular, the black box, personal variables, and complex models are used by marketers to analyze why consumers make the choices that they make.

5. Marketers use focus groups and surveys and track sales to better understand consumers' attitudes and perceptions of products and services. They use this information to create ad campaigns about existing and new products with the intention of creating a demand for products and services.

Key Terms

Consumer Buying Behaviour: It is the study of the ways of buying and disposing of goods, services, ideas, or experiences by the individuals, groups, and organizations in order to satisfy their needs and wants.

Cultural Factors: Factors exert a broad and deep influence on consumer behaviour and marketers need to understand the role played by the buyer's culture and subculture.

Focus Groups: Gather several consumers together at the same time and place asking them questions about how they feel about existing or new products.

Personal Factors: Characteristics that are specific to a person.

Psychological Factors: These are unique to a consumer's thought process.

Social Factors: These are quite diverse and can include a person's family, social interaction, work or school communities, or any group of people a person affiliates with or looks up to.

Surveys: Ask people for input that allows the marketing group to understand how consumers feel, what they want, and how they will react.

The Complex or Comprehensive Model: It considers all the internal and external stimuli when studying purchasing behaviour.

The Personal Variable Model: It studies what internal factors affect consumer behaviour and purchasing decisions, like personal opinions, belief systems, lifestyle, values, traditions, and goals.

The Stimulus-Response Model: It looks at environmental stimuli, such as economics, technology, and culture, combined with marketing stimuli, like the product, price, and promotion.

Tracking sales history and past consumer behaviour helps to predict future consumer behaviour.

Answers to Practice

What Is Consumer Behaviour?
1. d 2. d 3. b 4. a 5. a

Why Is Consumer Behaviour Important for Marketers?
1. a 2. d 3. d 4. c 5. a

What Affects Consumer Behaviour?
1. a 2. c 3. d 4. c 5. d

Consumer Behaviour Models
1. a 2. c 3. b 4. a 5. b

How Consumer Behaviour Is Studied?
1. a 2. b 3. b 4. a 5. b

References

Babin, B., Harris, E., Kyle, B., Murray, C.B. (2009). Canadian Edition. Nelson Education.

Kolm, J. (April, 2017). Check it out: Tim Hortons gets in with the coffee snobs. *Strategy Magazine*.

Kotler, P. and Keller, K. (2011) "Marketing Management" (14th edition), London: Pearson Education.

Vend. (July 28, 2017). 12 Forecasts for the retail industry in 2017. Retrieved from https://www.vendhq.com/uk/university/retail-trends-and-predictions-2017.

Yohn, D.L. (August, 2013). Don't forget gen Z. QSR Magazine. Retrieved from https://www.qsrmagazine.com/denise-lee-yohn/don-t-forget-gen-z.

5 Segmentation

LEARNING OBJECTIVES

LO1 Define and differentiate between market, market segment, and market segmentation

LO2 Identify the advantages and disadvantages of mass marketing

LO3 Explain the purpose of market segmentation to marketers

LO4 Differentiate between no market and fully segmented market segmentation

LO5 List the benefits of market segmentation

LO6 Describe and differentiate the four segmentation segments

LEARN...

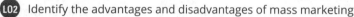

- *Is Tesla the ideal transportation–even battery powered– vehicle for everyone?*
- *Are the Toronto Maple Leafs Canada's favourite hockey team?*
- *Do all Canadians bank with the "Big 5" or do some prefer the community values of a credit union?*

Obviously one size does not fit all, and in today's marketing world, managers have realized the value of *segmenting* a mass market into smaller more specific customer groups that allow them to cater almost specifically, to the individual needs and wants of their customers.

It is important for marketing managers to understand the value of segmenting a mass market into smaller more specific groups and the criteria that are required for successful segmentation. *Segmentation* or the segmenting of a market is a strategy taken on by marketers which divides a mass market into subsets with distinct and common needs, interests, and priorities. Once divided, marketers design and implement *segmentation strategies* to better target these (often smaller but similar) customer segments.

These *strategies* allow marketers a better chance at achieving their business and marketing objectives, as well as an opportunity to collect insights and information that will help to identify and distinguish customers based on a variety of criteria.

By honing in and marketing to different customer segments, marketers are able to almost customize their marketing and yield greater response rates, stronger relationships with their target audience, and a better return on their investment (ROI).

What Is Marketing Segmentation?

 LO1 Define and differentiate between market, market segment, and market segmentation

 LO2 Identify the advantages and disadvantages of mass marketing

Not everyone likes all our flavours but each flavour is someone's favourite.

(Irv Robins founding partner of Baskin-Robbins)

If chocolate or vanilla were the only flavours available at your neighbourhood ice cream parlour, then Baskin-Robbins would probably not be in business. Burt Baskin and Irv Robbins believed that people should be able to try a variety of flavours until they found the one they wanted to buy. They believed that each customer was unique and made it their mission to appeal to the tastes of everyone. The company differentiates itself by appealing and marketing to the appetites of their customers with a rotating assortment of 31 different ice cream and non-milk flavour treats. Flavours like Moose Tracks (sugar-free), Vanilla Yogurt (fat-free) and Rainbow Sherbet (lactose-free) are just some of the 500 stock flavours that have been developed by Baskin-Robbins to appease their customers throughout the world.

Is ice cream the perfect dessert product for every Baskin-Robbins customer? How about milkshakes or ice cream cakes or specific non-dairy lifestyle and dietary needs? Given the available choices to consumers, marketers and their products need to be tailored to a specific customer within the market, making market segmentation a more appealing alternative to **mass marketing**.

Market and Market Segment

A **market** (or mass market) is made up of people or organizations who have the ability to purchase a product or service. In today's world, mass markets have splintered into smaller segments making it difficult for companies to practice mass marketing. A market can be further broken down into **market segments** which provide the marketer with a clearer picture of customers' needs and the chance to offer products and services that suit them. For example, people who are looking to purchase a new car are in the car buyer's market. If you were to segment your car buyer's market and identify those new car buyers who have families, you would most likely market Mini Van, SUV, MPV, and/or hatchback vehicles to them.

Market Segmentation

A marketer segmenting a market or **market segmentation** will divide the market into smaller groups of buyers with distinct needs, characteristics, or behaviour who might require separate products or marketing mixes.

The Difference Between Mass Marketing and Market Segmentation

As opposed to *mass marketing* where marketers direct their activities to the entire market, *market segmentation* allows marketers the opportunity to divide a market into several smaller groups (or segments) and to offer these groups tailored campaigns and products. For companies to successfully reach their ideal "true blue" customer, they need to divide or "segment" the market into similar and identifiable groups.

Advantages of Mass Marketing

- Large market potential
- Lowest costs
- Economy of scale
- Higher profit margin through economy of scale

Disadvantages of Mass Marketing

- Difficult to practice mass marketing in a diversified and splintered customer market
- Difficult to create a single product that appeals to all diverse groups in the mass market

Advantages of Segment Marketing

- The marketer may face fewer competitors
- The marketer is more efficient while serving a defined market segment
- The marketer can market more effectively by fine-tuning its products, prices, and programs to the needs of a carefully defined segment

Segmentation of Drinking Water Market

Source: Chris Nuzzaco/Moment/Getty Images

Practice...

1. What best describes the definition of a market segment?
   a. Every consumer in the market
   b. Consumers who are looking to buy a home
   c. Francophone Canadians who live in the province of Ontario
   d. Francophone Canadians

2. Market segmentation is the process of dividing a market into distinct groups or segments that share _____ characteristics.
   a. common
   b. opposite
   c. conflicting
   d. mass

3. Women between the ages of 35–44 living in the 416 area code and who enjoy martial arts is an example of a:
   a. mass market audience.
   b. segment of the female market.
   c. segment of the female martial arts market in Canada.
   d. specific segment of the female martial arts market in the city of Toronto.

4. Canadian males from P.E.I. who like the Toronto Maple Leafs is best described as an example of a _____.
   a. mass market segment
   b. hockey fan segment
   c. Canadian male hockey fan segment market
   d. segment of fans within the Toronto Maple Leaf fan database

5. An example of a Starbucks mass marketing campaign would be:
   a. an email to Starbucks customers introducing the new triple light Decaf Mocha Frappuccino.
   b. a text message communicating the opening of a new store location two blocks down the street from a customer.
   c. the announcement of a new rewards program on television.
   d. the placement of an ad in a health magazine announcing a new diet drink.

Apply...

1. Let's say you own an ice cream shop called "Scoop" in downtown Montreal where you make your own delicious flavours in house. Your customers love your products and go beyond the traditional vanilla and chocolate flavours often ordering flavours like Chocolate Chip, Burnt Marshmallow, or Blueberry. Others prefer your "Scoop" sherbet products as a healthy alternative to ice cream and some are seasonal ice cream lovers and prefer to only enjoy your treat in the summer months but come in to purchase ice cream cakes for seasonal special occasions.

   As the owner and marketing manager of "Scoops" ...

   - Identify your market. Be as detailed as possible.

   _____

   _____

   _____

   _____

   _____

   _____

   _____

   _____

   - Segment your market into at least five groups. Be as detailed and descriptive as possible.

   _____

   _____

   _____

   _____

   _____

   _____

   _____

   _____

   - Develop a newspaper ad for the local newspaper, inviting two of these segments to come to "Scoops".
     ◊ What would you say?
     ◊ What types of visuals would you use?

   _____

   _____

   _____

   _____

   _____

   _____

   _____

   _____

Why Is Market Segmentation Important?

 Explain the purpose of market segmentation to marketers

 Differentiate between no market and fully segmented market segmentation

List the benefits of market segmentation

> *Not everyone likes all our flavours but each flavour is someone's favourite.*

(Irv Robins founding partner of Baskin Robbins)

Purpose of Market Segmentation

Most companies today segment their markets into similar groups. By taking such an approach, marketers create an almost customized experience for their customers, gain a stronger and loyal following, and reap a more significant ROI.

For example, when Whole Foods Supermarkets started, they realized that not everyone would purchase their expensive organic produce and premium labelled products. They switched strategy and decided not to exhaust their marketing budget on mass advertising but to focus on a segmented market of "organic supermarket shoppers". Rather than reaching out to those who preferred "Big Box" retailers, they decided to segment the market based on demographics such as age and income, as well as the consumers' price sensitivity and their appetite for healthy living and organic products.

As a result, their target market consisted of adult males and females aged 25–44, with a household income of $65,000+, who live downtown, are physically active, have healthy eating habits, grow a garden in their backyard, and shop at farmer's markets.

Based on this more segmented and targeted strategy, their marketing creative took on a new face and utilized younger, more active, and healthier looking models in their creative. Their media plan focused on local urban magazines like *Now Magazine*, social media platforms like Pinterest, and email blasts that were formulated with age and income specifics. They also partnered with local gyms like Goodlife and allowed gym-goers to sample their healthy produce and menu items.

When it comes to reaching a market, marketers have numerous choices at their disposal.

They can *mass-market* and direct their marketing activities to the entire market. They can *segment* a market and tailor to the needs and wants of a particular market segment on the basis of gender, geography, income, lifestyle, ethnicity, family life cycle, or age. They can even **fully segment a market** to the point where individuals receive customized messages and offers.

Why Is Segmentation Important to Marketers?

Companies will probably not survive, if their marketing strategy is dependent on mass marketing. Market segmentation allows a business to precisely reach a consumer with specific needs and wants. In the long run, this *benefits customers with products that are specifically catered to their needs.*

As for *marketers, their organization benefits twofold:*

- They are able to use their limited resources more effectively and allow better strategic marketing decisions.

- By creating products that are specifically catered to their customers' needs and wants, they create a loyal base and following of customers and a potential greater return on their marketing investment (ROI).

For example, Whole Foods will not waste their marketing dollars on expensive Super Bowl ads when they know that the market segment they appeal to is very specific. By knowing their segment, their marketing dollars are used effectively, and they are able to communicate with a segment that has been identified as a heavy user of organic products and one who is willing to pay more for their brand.

The Benefits of Market Segmentation

- It provides customers with products and services that specifically cater to them.

- It reduces risk marketers because they know where, when, how, and to whom a product or service will be marketed.

- It increases marketing efficiency because the marketer understands the designated segment's characteristics and is consistent and focused when messaging to them.

- It creates a loyal customer base (Boundless, 2016).

 **Practice...**

1. Which two points below are benefits of market segmentation?
   a. Allows the business to sell less products overall and perhaps decrease profit.
   b. Allows customers to feel that their needs are being better catered to.
   c. Prevents products from being promoted to the wrong audience, otherwise which may result in resources being wasted and possible losses.
   d. Allows a business to target particular groups with particular products.

2. In Saturday's National Newspaper, Whole Foods advertised across the country "OUR FRESH ORGANIC PRODUCE IS HERE CANADA!!!" This is an example of:
   a. full market segmentation.
   b. no market segmentation.
   c. differentiation.
   d. segmentation.

3. On Saturday, Whole Foods advertised in every local newspaper across Canada that "OUR FRESH ORGANIC PRODUCE IS HERE (name of local town)!!!" This is an example of:
   a. full market segmentation.
   b. no market segmentation.
   c. differentiation.
   d. segmentation.

4. An example of mass marketing communication to consumers is:
   a. a promotional health event at a local hospital.
   b. radio advertisements for gym memberships to females demographics only.
   c. a direct mail piece addressed to homeowners who are looking to sell their home.
   d. a television ad on tonight's 6 pm news.

 **Apply...**

1. Cineplex Odeon is showing the new *Pirates of the Caribbean: Dead Men Tell No Tales* film at their theatres. The price to see the film varies based on age:

    *   Child (3–13 years of age)
    *   Senior (65+ years of age)
    *   General admission (14–64 years of age)

    The prices also varied based on their viewing choice:

    *   3D
    *   3D Box AVX
    *   VIP

    Finally movie goers were asked if they wanted a Super Ticket, which allowed them to purchase a digital version of the movie they were going to view. The prices for each of these choices varied from $13.99 to $46.84.

    Based on the information above:

    *   In groups of four people, develop a *no market segmentation* email campaign for Cineplex Odeon.
    *   What would you say to your consumers?

    _____

    _____

    _____

    _____

    _____

    _____

    _____

    _____

    _____

    _____

    _____

    _____

    _____

    _____

    _____

    _____

    _____

    _____

    _____

    _____

to be continued

 **Apply...**

continued

2. Based on the information above, and in your same groups, develop a *full market segmentation* email campaign for Cineplex Odeon:

- Identify who your segments are.
- What type of medium and creativity would you use?
- What would you say to each group to entice them to come and see the movie?

_____
_____
_____
_____
_____
_____
_____
_____
_____
_____
_____
_____
_____
_____
_____
_____
_____
_____
_____
_____
_____
_____
_____
_____
_____

Types of Market Segments

LO6 Describe and differentiate the four segmentation segments

- Geographic
- Demographic
- Psychographic
- Behavioural

You can divide a market into segments based on the following four categories (Table 5.1):

Geographic segmentation is where a market is divided up based upon geographic differences between consumers. Your potential customers will have different needs based on the geography they are located in. You can geographically segment a market by cities, counties, regions, and international regions. You can also break a market down into rural, suburban, and urban areas. Certain foods, for example, have very specific geographic interest in the United States Grits, for instance, are common in the South and Southeast regions. In the summer of 2016, McDonald's Canada Great Canadian Taste Adventure created a trans-Canadian menu filled with regional Canadian dishes that included everything from poutine to represent Quebec, to barbecue burgers for the west, lobster rolls for the east and Nanaimo sundaes to represent the West Coast. This is an example of regional segmentation based on geographic consumer preferences and product availability.

Source: Muskoka Stock Photos/Shutterstock

TABLE 5.1   Segmentation segments

Geographic	Demographic	Psychographic	Behavioural

• Customer Location
• Area Code
• Province
• Region/ Location
	• Age
	• Gender
	• Ethnicity
	• Income
	  ◇ Occupation
	  ◇ Socio– economic group
		• Personality
		• Lifestyle
		• Attitudes
		• Class
			• Product Usage
			• Buying Pattern
			• Decision Makers
			• Decision Attributes
			• Customer Attitude

Source: Based on Armstrong, Kotler, Trifts, Buchwitz. (2018). Marketing, An Introduction (Updated 6th Canadian Edition with Integrated B2B Case). Pearson Canada.

Demographic segmentation divides a market based upon demographic differences between consumers, such as age, gender, race, and income. An example of a demographic market segment is white males between the age of 45 and 55 years with gross annual incomes between $75,000 and $125,000. The idea is that consumers with certain demographic characteristics will have specific needs and wants and should be targeted differently than groups with different demographic characteristics.

Age	Gender	Race	Income
34 years	Male	Caucasian	$55K

Source: Hero Images/Getty Images

Psychographic segmentation is where you divide the market based upon consumer traits, attitudes, interests, or lifestyles. People have different interests, attitudes, and traits. Some people really care about the environment, while others don't. Some people are very fitness and health conscious while others are foodies. Some people take sports very seriously, while some just want to have some fun on the weekends. Psychographic segmentation occurs when you break your market down along these interests and attitudes so you can market the appropriate product to each segment of the market. For example, an organic supermarket like Whole Foods may divide its market into consumers who are primarily interested in the environmental advantages of organic farming, consumers who are primarily interested in the health benefits of organic food, and consumers that seem to just be buying organic food because it's the current thing to do. Different marketing approaches would be used with each of these markets. Another example—an automobile company may decide to segment their market into consumers who are interested in luxury, consumers who are interested in practicality, and consumers who are interested in the environment. As a result, you focus your product design and marketing of luxury sedans on one segment (luxury), station wagons and SUVs on another segment (practicality), and your electric hybrids on the environmentally-conscious market segment.

Age	Gender	Race	Income	Lifestyle
34 years	Male	Caucasian	$55K	Party Animal

Source: Hero Images/Getty Images

Behavioural segmentation divides the customer base into groups based on the way they respond to promotions, price changes, and the channels they use to communicate. Based on behavioural segmentation, consumers can be grouped aligned with any of various business strategies such as:

- **Product Usage:** Rather than offering one's product as a direct replacement for a similar or competitive product, it may be useful to segment customers based on benefits that she seeks for in a product thereby intensifying its relevance.

- **Buying Pattern:** This includes recency, frequency, and monetary (RFM) value of purchase, channel used, day/time of purchase, etc.

- **Decision Makers:** This involves understanding people behind the decision-making process.
  - ◊ Is the customer influenced by online reviews/opinions or does she rely on feedback from friends within social networks or act on opinions within the family?

- **Decision Attributes:** The criteria can include price, preference to self-service, quality of product, service quality, approachability, events in customer lifecycle, etc.

- **Customer Attitude:** This may include customer's readiness to purchase, risk appetite (early adopter, early majority, late majority), brand loyalty, etc.

Practice...

1. How many types of market segmentation are there?
   a. One
   b. Two
   c. Three
   d. Four

2. Name the different types of market segments.
   a. Demographic, Geographic, Psychographic, Social
   b. Geographic, Psychographic, Behavioural, Biological
   c. Demographic, Geographic, Psychographic, Behavioural
   d. Demographic, Psychographic, Chronological, Behavioural

3. Which is an example of demographic segmentation (gender)?
   a. Walmart's generic brand
   b. Perfume
   c. Toothpaste
   d. Diapers

4. Which is not an example of geographic segmentation?
   a. 416 area code
   b. Children aged 5–14
   c. French-speaking Quebecers
   d. Males who like to play soccer

5. Which is the best example of psychographic segmentation?
   a. Teenagers who live in the United Kingdom
   b. Females 55+ with a household income of $100K who drive SUVs
   c. Parents of toddlers
   d. People who live in Vancouver and make $50K

 **Apply...**

1. The Toronto Raptors basketball team would like to increase the number of Raptors team jerseys that they sell. They have fans from all over the world and from all walks of life (https://tinyurl.com/flextext-rank-nba-teams). Currently on Ranker, they are fifth most popular in the NBA! As marketing manager for the Raptors, you are asked to segment your fan base according to geography, demography, psychography, and behaviour. Describe what customers in each segment would look like. Here is some more information to help you: https://tinyurl.com/flextext-raptors and https://tinyurl.com/flextext-raptors-fans

KNOW...

Learning Objectives

1. Market segmentation is the process of dividing a broad consumer or business market, normally consisting of existing and potential customers, into sub-groups of consumers (known as segments) based on some type of shared characteristics.

2. Advantages of mass marketing include large market potential, lowest costs, economies of scale, and higher profit margin through economy of scale. It is difficult to practice mass marketing in a diversified and splintered customer market and to create a single product that appeals to all diverse groups in the mass market. With segmented marketing, a marketer may face fewer competitors, will be more efficient while serving a defined market segment, and can market more effectively by fine-tuning its products, prices, and programs to the needs of carefully defined segment.

3. Market segmentation allows a business to precisely reach a consumer with specific needs and wants. In the long run, this benefits customers with products that are specifically catered to their needs. By taking on segmentation, marketers are able to use their limited resources more effectively and allow better strategic marketing decisions and the opportunity to create products that are specifically catered to their customers' needs and wants.

4. There are four types of segments that markets usually divide customers by—geography, demography, psychography, and consumer behaviour.

Key Terms

Behavioural Segmentation: Divides the customer base into groups based on the way they respond to promotions, price changes, and the channels they use to communicate.

Demographic Segmentation: Divides a market up based upon demographic differences between consumers, such as age, gender, race, and income.

Full Market Segmentation: Segmenting a market to the point where individuals receive customized messages and offers.

Geographic Segmentation: Where a market is divided up based upon geographic differences between consumers.

Market: People or organizations with needs, wants, and the ability to buy a product or service. A market can be further broken down into segments. For example, everyone needs water to drink and survive—hence the water market.

Market Segment: A subgroup of people or organizations who share one or more characteristics that cause them to have similar product needs. For example, everyone needs water to drink, but does everyone need bottled water or premium (more expensive) bottled water? (See Page 85.)

Market Segmentation: The process of dividing a market with common needs into meaningful, relatively similar, identifiable segments or groups like gender, geography, income, lifestyle, ethnicity, family life cycle, or age.

Mass Marketing: An attempt to appeal to an entire market with one basic marketing strategy utilizing mass distribution and mass media.

Psychographic Segmentation: Where a market is divided based upon consumer traits, attitudes, interests, or lifestyles.

Answers to Practice

What Is Marketing Segmentation?
1. c 2. a 3. d 4. d 5. c

Why Is Market Segmentation Important?
1. b 2. b 3. d 4. d

Types of Market Segments
1. d 2. c 3. b 4. c 5. b

References

Armstrong, Kotler, Trifts, Buchwitz. (2018). *Marketing, An Introduction* (Updated 6th Canadian Edition with Integrated B2B Case). Pearson Canada.

Boundless. "The Importance of Market Segmentation." Boundless Marketing Boundless, 20 Sep. 2016. Retrieved 22 Jan. 2017 from https://www.boundless.com/marketing/textbooks/boundless-marketing-textbook/consumer-marketing-4/market-segmentation-36/the-importance-of-market-segmentation-187-4063/.

6 Targeting

LEARNING OBJECTIVES

LO1 Learn Porter's Five Forces model and how it is used to assess a market before marketing strategy commences

LO2 Learn other factors that affect the selection of a market segment

LO3 Define target market

LO4 Understand the importance of target marketing in marketing strategy

LO5 Differentiate the different types of strategies used to select a target market

LO6 Identify the factors influencing the choice of the market targeting strategy

LO7 Know the different approaches used to define and reach your target market

LEARN...

Until not too long ago, most companies and business owners thought it was enough to market their products and services to the "Adult 18–54 year old" consumer market.

Age no longer means what it used to. Today, people say things like "50 is the new 30" and "40 is the new 20", and baby boomers are into fitness, second careers, new technology, and all sorts of social media applications. Teens and Tweens are brand savvy, media, and tech sophisticated and prefer communication via Snapchat and Instagram versus all other traditional communication channels. Thirty year olds may still be living at home with their parents and have come to the realization that they "live and enjoy the moment" versus having a car or a place of their own in the near future. Last but not least, people today are repeating stages and recycling their lives. You can have two men who are 64 years old—one retired and driving around in a Winnebago—while the other has just remarried and living with a toddler in his downtown condominium.

Today, the homogeneous "18–54" market is no longer around.

Today's market is competitive and hard to enter. If you're already in, it's hard to stay afloat. Consumers are diverse, connected, savvy, and sophisticated. They don't like to be lumped with everyone else and to talk about them in any kind of general way is not only a misconception but a business and marketing faux pas.

Marketers of today have a tough job and they have to be very strategic in their selection of a target market and audience.

First, they have to assess and decide whether the market they are entering is "ripe for the picking". And then, they have to determine whether to market or to socioeconomic status or to ethnicity or to gender or to region or to lifestyle or to technological sophistication. There's no end to the number of different strategies a marketer can take on to slice today's target audience pie.

This is but a snapshot of today's consumer. What used to be normal, no longer is and to take a "one size fits all" approach to your marketing, will affect the relationship that you have with the people that are most likely to buy from you, have a relationship with you, and promote and endorse your brand. Therefore, as marketers build their strategies for success, it's important for them to understand the type of market they are entering, who their target market is, what sets them apart from everyone else, and how to effectively reach them.

Evaluating if the Market Segment Is a Good Fit

 Learn Porter's Five Forces model and how it is used to assess a market before marketing strategy commences

LO2 Learn other factors that affect the selection of a market segment

Business strategy focuses on how a firm competes within a particular market or industry.

Before commencing strategy and selecting the best target audience, marketers need to assess and diagnose if the organization has the ability to compete among other brands, and if they wield a competitive advantage over their competition. According to Porter, there are "five forces" that may impede or expedite success in the market (Figure 1):

- **Competitors**
  - ◊ How many direct or indirect competitors have access to the customer?
  - ◊ Is there one very dominant player or are all equal in strength/size?

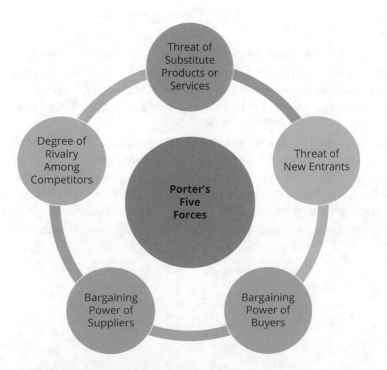

FIGURE 1 Porter's Five Forces model.

Source: Based on Porter, M. (March-April, 1979). How competitive forces shape strategy. *Harvard Business Review*, 57, 86–89.

- **New Entrants**

  ◊ How easy or difficult is it for new entrants to enter the market and start to compete?

  ◊ How easy is it for a competitor to access customers?

- **Substitute Products**

  ◊ How easy can our product or service be substituted, especially cheaper?

- **Relative Power of Buyers**

  ◊ How strong is the position of buyers?

  ◊ What type of bargaining power does the segment (consumer or business) have in terms of affecting the 4 P's?

- **Relative Power of Suppliers**

  ◊ How many suppliers are there and how much power do they have?

  ◊ Do they have the ability to effectively supply product to consumers?

  ◊ Is there a monopoly in the category?

The Five Forces model is a reality check which helps marketers to assess the attractiveness and influencers of the market and the opportunity for the business to succeed. The weaker these five forces are, the greater the opportunity will be for a brand or company to succeed. Vice versa, the stronger these forces are, the more difficult it will be to perform effectively and to get the best results from the market.

Marketers also need to evaluate different segments of the population and assess if the segment is a good fit. The three things marketers look at are:

- The segment's size and growth

- The segment's structural attractiveness

- The ability of the company's to fulfill their objectives with the right resources

In order to evaluate segments, the company needs to collect and analyse relevant data on current segment sales, growth rates, and anticipated profitability of segments. But even if we have these data, what is the right size and the right growth for our company? The largest or fastest-growing ones? Or small niche segments?

There is no answer that applies to every company. Larger and faster growing segments may not always be the most appealing to the market. They may require too much effort and time, may not be profitable, and/or may require added resources. Marketing management's objective, therefore, is to design strategies that align with their corporate objectives, differentiate them from the competition, and allow them to build strong and profitable relationships with consumers.

Practice...

1. Which of the following is not an element of Porter's Five Forces model?
   a. The potential competition from new entrants
   b. The firm's macroeconomic environment
   c. The bargaining power of suppliers
   d. The firm's existing competition

2. In Porter's Five Forces, the "threat of new entrants" relates to:
   a. barriers to entry.
   b. substitutes.
   c. switching costs.
   d. buyer power.

3. Porter's Value Chain is essentially a tool for:
   a. calculating what a firm is worth.
   b. identifying the competitive forces within an industry.
   c. advising firms on how to price their products.
   d. diagnosing and enhancing sources of competitive advantage within an organization.

4. Business strategy focuses on:
   a. how a firm competes within a particular market or industry.
   b. where a firm is going and the scope of its activities.
   c. strategies related to functional areas such as marketing, production, and HRM.
   d. how a firm competes within a particular market or industry.

5. A market would be difficult to enter if there is:
   a. wide access to distribution channels.
   b. patented or proprietary know how.
   c. common technology.
   d. low brand loyalty.

Apply...

1. Working in groups, consider the following: You're a manufacturing company who create e-books on behalf of textbook publishing companies. Basically you put the books into a digital format on behalf of textbook publishers. The e-books are used by Canadian post-secondary institutions. Where would you place the following five statements on the Five Forces model? Hint: These points could potentially go in more than one of the five forces. The five points to consider are that:

    *   It is easy to set up an e-manufacturing company to create digital (electronic) books.

    *   Students have easy and cheap access to hardcopy textbooks, online videos, and paper-based learning materials.

    *   Smartphone manufacturers are investing heavily in improved touch screens and e-reader software.

    *   Price comparison websites have increased in number.

    *   Another e-reader manufacturer has signed an exclusive deal with a publishing company.

_____

_____

_____

_____

_____

_____

_____

_____

_____

_____

_____

_____

_____

_____

to be continued

 **Apply…**

continued

2. In groups, develop marketing strategies for the e-book reader manufacturer to improve its competitive position in the e-reader market for each of the five points above.

_____

_____

_____

_____

_____

_____

_____

_____

_____

_____

_____

_____

_____

_____

_____

_____

_____

_____

_____

_____

_____

_____

_____

_____

_____

_____

_____

_____

_____

_____

_____

_____

Selecting Target Market Segments

 L03 Define target market

L04 Understand the importance of target marketing in marketing strategy

What Is a Target Market?

Imagine that you are the marketing manager for a hot sauce like *Tabasco*.

You've conducted your market analysis and have found that you are losing market share to some new private label brands. The market still loves your product and is ready for some new flavours and varieties. You have some ideas on what your marketing should look and feel like and even some packaging and design concepts to set your new products apart from others. But, do you know to whom you're marketing and how to go about in finding your ideal target market?

Here are some questions you the marketer might ask:

- What gender do you reach out to . . . Males or Females?

  - So you decide on females. That might be too big of an audience and you may alienate some—*you still need to chip away and finesse your target.*

- Where do they live? An urban or rural environment? What country?

  - So they are females, who live in Winnipeg Manitoba. That may differentiate your customer a bit more and help you with your distribution or even media plans—*but it is still too broad.*

- What's their household income?

  - So they are females, who live in Winnipeg Manitoba with a household income of below $50,000 annually. This might help us figure out if the consumer can afford our product and what they're willing to spend—*getting closer though.*

- Do they have an appetite for hot sauce? If so, how hot do they prefer their sauce?

  - So they are females, who live in Winnipeg Manitoba with a household income of below $50,000 annually, who like their hot sauce extra hot. This will help us to narrow it down a bit more and identify the true lovers of a locally sourced hot sauce.

- What type of food do they serve it on?

  - So they are females, who live in Winnipeg Manitoba with a household income of below $50,000 annually, who like their hot sauce extra hot, who like to apply their hot sauce on everything from pasta to pizza. This will help us to further market the product experience with recipe recommendations or restaurant partnerships.

These questions (and many more) are asked in order to better target those who are most interested or a better fit for your product or service. It is a more effective and finessed strategy versus marketing to everyone which will most likely be inefficient and expensive and could provide the marketing manager and the organization with an opportunity to effectively compete with other competing brands.

According to Armstrong et al. (2017), a **target market** is defined as:

> *A set of buyers sharing common needs or characteristics that the company decides to serve.*

A target market is the *customer or organization* that will ultimately buy a company's products or services. As a marketer, the target market is the person or company that you will design products and marketing programs for. In the case of Tabasco hot sauce, a target market may be, for example, males who enjoy hot sauce or a bit of heat with their foods.

Source: Andrei Kuzmik/Shutterstock.

Who Is the Perfect Target Audience for Tabasco Brand Pepper Sauce?

A **target market analysis** is a systematic and comprehensive assessment that allows you to identify important characteristics about your target market and group them into categories based on those characteristics. Segmenting the market in this way not only identifies the customers who are most likely to buy your product, it also identifies the best way to reach them. This knowledge lets an organization to focus their resources where they are most likely to get the largest return on their investment.

When breaking down the target market, the most basic variables used to better identify the target market are demographics, geography, and psychographics.

When breaking down the target market, some basic demographic questions that allow you to identify the target market include:

- What is their age?
- What is their gender?

- What is their occupation?
- What is their income?
- What is their marital status?
- What is their ethnicity?
- What is their level of education?
- What is their religion?

When breaking down the target market, some basic geographic questions that allow you to identify the target market include:

- Where do your potential customers live?
- Will they travel to buy your product?
- What's the climate where they live?

When breaking down the target market, some basic psychographic questions that allow you to identify the target market include:

- What are their lifestyle, values, attitudes, and beliefs.
- What are their interests and hobbies?
- Why will they buy your product?

Practice...

1. Which of the following statements is true?
   a. A target market is a set of buyers that the company decides to serve who do not share common needs or characteristics.
   b. A target market is a set of buyers that the company decides to serve who share common needs or characteristics.
   c. A company cannot be a target market.
   d. A consumer cannot be a target market.

2. Effective target marketing will:
   a. generate the best candidates for a position in the marketing department.
   b. reach a mass audience.
   c. allow for a greater return on your marketing investment.
   d. reach those who are apprehensive or on the fence about your product.

3. Which of the following criteria would most likely not help you to find your target audience, if you were a marketer of a diet soft drink product?
   a. Level of fitness
   b. Gender
   c. Product usage
   d. Place of employment

4. The premise of _____ is to identify market segments, select one or more, and develop products and marketing mixes tailored to each selected segment.
   a. mass marketing
   b. product-variety marketing
   c. macromarketing
   d. target marketing

5. A target market analysis is:
   a. a test of the market to assess what the competition is doing.
   b. an assessment that allows the marketer to identify important characteristics about the target market.
   c. very similar to a SWOT analysis.
   d. an assessment that allows the marketer the chance to see how many suppliers exist in the market.

 **Apply...**

1. Individually, create a profile of one ideal target customer (or organization) for Swell Water bottles (https://www.swellbottle.com/). Use your imagination. Describe the ideal target customer including why he or she buys, what his or her problem is, how old, economic status, family status, favourite media, and where you might find this person to send a message.

_____

_____

_____

_____

_____

_____

_____

_____

_____

_____

_____

_____

_____

_____

_____

_____

_____

_____

_____

_____

_____

_____

_____

_____

_____

_____

_____

_____

_____

_____

_____

_____

to be continued

 **Apply...**

continued

2. In groups of two, define your partner's target market profile. Make sure you incorporate the demographic, geographic, and psychographic variables that identify your partner.

Demographic	
What is your:	
Age	
Gender	
Occupation	
Income	
Marital Status	
Ethnicity	
Level of education	
Religion	
Geographic	
Where do you live in the summer time	
What's the climate like?	
Where do you travel to buy most of your consumable goods? (that is, groceries etc.)	
Psychographic	
What is your preferred:	
Lifestyle	
Values	
Attitudes	
Beliefs	
Interests	
Hobbies	

Selecting Target Market Segments

L05 Differentiate the different types of strategies used to select a target market

Target market selection can be carried out in a variety of ways by companies.

You can take on an **undifferentiated** or **mass marketing** strategy and focus on the common needs of the whole market rather than on what is different of its consumers. Unfortunately, taking this approach has its limitations because it is near impossible to satisfy all consumers with the same product, service, or marketing approach.

Most large companies divide a large target audience into smaller sets of consumers with common wants, needs, and interests, and take on a **differentiated** or **segmented strategy**.

This approach will enable you to design, promote, and market in a way that targets specific groups or segments within your market differently. For instance, a car company produces several different models of cars, and often even offers different brands. General Motors, for example, consists of more than the core Chevy brand and targets its own segment of car buyers with brands like Cadillac, Buick, and Corvette. In the Tabasco hot sauce example, Tabasco offers a variety of different flavours besides its original version so that it can reach the various consumer spice palettes that exist. The differentiated approach is lauded by many marketing professionals but can be costly when developing several marketing plans for the several segments that may exist.

Differentiated / Segmented Marketing Approach

Source: Prachaya Roekdeethaweesab/Shutterstock.

Tabasco has segmented their audience and offers them a variety of flavours besides the original recipe. This approach leaves the marketer with more than one brand and product to offer in a variety communication media outlets.

Segmentation in the Greeting Card Category

Source: ValeStock/Shutterstock.

Greeting card companies segment their audiences by characteristics such as age, stage of life, family status, occasion, and ethnicity, to the point where no two cards on the rack are alike.

Another strategy to take on is a **niche** or **concentrated marketing strategy**. As a strategy, niche marketing is aimed at being a big fish in a small pond instead of being a small fish in a big pond. With this approach, you concentrate all your marketing efforts on a small but specific and well-defined segment of the population. This enables you to market and price your products more efficiently to only those consumers that will provide you with the best returns. The difference between a niche and a differentiated segment is the size. While a segment is rather large and will in most cases attract several competitors, a niche is quite small and may be focused on by few competitors only. A niche approach allows new entrants and smaller companies to focus their limited resources on serving niches. The key is to find those niches that are overlooked by larger competitors.

The last strategy to take on is a **micromarketing strategy**. Micromarketing is the practice of tailoring products and marketing efforts to suit the individual tastes of a small and specific group. This segmented group could be so small that it could consist of only one person—also known as *individual marketing* or a small geographic area—also known as *local marketing*. In micromarketing, relationships with the few customers the company focuses on is of utmost importance. The company can simply not afford to lose one of the few, but highly profitable customers. With advances in manufacturing and production and new communications technology, social network companies like Groupon and Living Social are using micromarketing strategies to target specific individuals, neighbourhoods, and communities in urban and rural markets across Canada (Figure 2).

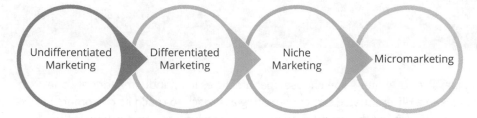

FIGURE 2 Target marketing strategies.

Source: Based on Kotler, A., Buchwitz, T. (2017). *Marketing: An Introduction*, Pearson Canada; 253.

Practice...

1. A company who develops a single marketing mix for the whole market and doesn't segment the market, uses which of the following target marketing strategies?
   a. Niche Marketing
   b. Differentiated Marketing
   c. Undifferentiated Marketing
   d. Micromarketing

2. A company that divides a large target audience into smaller sets of consumers with common wants, needs, and interests, uses which of the following target marketing strategies?
   a. Niche Marketing
   b. Differentiated Marketing
   c. Undifferentiated Marketing
   d. Micromarketing

3. A company that concentrates all of their marketing efforts on a small but specific and well-defined segment of the population is known as:
   a. niche marketing.
   b. differentiated marketing.
   c. undifferentiated marketing.
   d. micromarketing.

4. The target marketing strategy that could reach a segmented group so small that it could consist of only one person, is better known as:
   a. niche marketing.
   b. differentiated marketing.
   c. undifferentiated marketing.
   d. micromarketing.

5. A _____ target marketing approach allows new entrants and smaller companies to focus their limited resources on serving niches. The key is to find those niches that are overlooked by larger competitors.
   a. Niche Marketing
   b. Differentiated Marketing
   c. Undifferentiated Marketing
   d. Micromarketing

 # Apply...

1. Review several beverage (soda, alcohol, water—you choose) manufactures in an industry. Identify one beverage company that has taken a differentiated target marketing approach to reach its customers in the industry of your choice. List off some of the products they offer to consumers. Identify who is the ideal target audience for the product(s) you choose?

    _____
    _____
    _____
    _____
    _____
    _____
    _____
    _____
    _____
    _____
    _____
    _____

2. Tabasco has three flavours of hot sauce. As the marketing manager for this company, develop a niche target marketing approach to reach out to consumers. Who would these consumers be and how would you communicate with them? You may have a different segment for each of the sauces.

Source: Prachaya Roekdeethaweesab/Shutterstock.

    _____
    _____
    _____
    _____
    _____
    _____
    _____
    _____
    _____

Choosing a Targeting Strategy

LO6 Identify the factors influencing the choice of the market targeting strategy

LO7 Know the different approaches used to define and reach your target market

Marketing segmentation teaches us that it is difficult for a company to serve all consumers in the market. The variety of customers and their needs is just too large. Therefore, marketers segment the market, by dividing it up into smaller differentiated, niche, or micromarketing segments (Figure 3).

Which market targeting strategy is chosen depends on many factors. None of the strategies above works best in every situation. Rather, the market targeting strategy depends on several characteristics of the company. When choosing a market targeting strategy, the company should consider:

- **The Company's Resources:** If resources are limited, a concentrated market targeting strategy might make more sense.

- **The Degree of Product Variability:** In case of uniform products, such as apples or steel, undifferentiated marketing may be more suited. In case of products that can vary in design (cars, cameras etc.), more narrow differentiation and concentration is suitable.

- **The Product Lifecycle:** When a company introduces a new product, it may be helpful to launch only one version. Undifferentiated or concentrated marketing might make sense the most. In the mature stage, a segmented market targeting may be appropriate.

- **Market Variability:** If you talk about a kind of product where all buyers have the same tastes, buy the same amounts etc., undifferentiated marketing makes sense.

- **Competitors' Marketing Strategies:** If competitors apply differentiated or concentrated market targeting strategies, using undifferentiated marketing may prove to be fatal. However, the firm might also gain an advantage by using a different market targeting strategy than competitors, especially if it can serve individual customers better by meeting their needs. Then, a concentrated market targeting strategy or micromarketing will work best.

Companies need to consider many factors when choosing a market—targeting strategy. Which strategy a company takes on depends on their financial and human resources, product variability, product life-cycle stage, market variability, and the marketing strategies of the competition. To determine who your best target market consists of, start by answering three basic questions:

- **What problem does your product or service solve?** Does it help soothe teething babies? Does it make men feel taller? Does it help companies to garner more publicity?

FIGURE 3 Market segmentation and strategy.

- **Who is most likely to have this problem?** In what situations do they use it? This is where you start breaking down who you should be focusing on. Is it individuals? Businesses? Families?

- **Are there different groups with different needs?** You may have more than one target market, or market segment, based on how they use a product or service. For example, a bike shop may help families with young children to choose a safe bike for their 5-year-old, while a 30-something athlete may want advice in choosing a professional racing bike.

Get a little more specific about what pain points your product or service addresses and then who typically feels that pain.

Once you are clear about who is most likely to need or want your product or service, the marketer needs to get even more specific about this group, or groups, of people. There are several different ways to define your target market, based on different characteristics. You should decide which approach comes closest to exactly describing your perfect customer:

- **Consumer or Business**
  - ◊ Is your customer a B2B (business-to-business) or B2C (business-to-consumer)?

- **Geographic**
  - ◊ Where do they live, work, vacation, or do business?

- **Demographic**
  - ◊ What is their gender, age, income level, education level, and marital status?

- **Psychographic**
  - ◊ What are their internal attitudes and values?

- **Generation**
  - ◊ What generation were they born in—Baby Boomers, Gen X, or Gen Y?

- **Life Stage**
  - ◊ What stage of life are they in? Post-college, retirement, newly married, newly divorced, or parenting young children?

- **Behavioural**
  - ◊ How often do they use your product or a similar product?

Armed with a clear understanding of your target market(s), a marketer can now begin to craft marketing messages that appeal to that particular group's pain points and preferences.

Practice...

1. Defining a target market based on where people shop is an example of:
   a. behavioural segmentation.
   b. psychographic segmentation.
   c. geographic segmentation.
   d. generational segmentation.

2. Defining a target market based on where they live is an example of:
   a. behavioural segmentation.
   b. psychographic segmentation.
   c. geographic segmentation.
   d. generational segmentation.

3. Defining a target market based on the number of years that they are married is an example of:
   a. demographic segmentation.
   b. psychographic segmentation.
   c. life stage segmentation.
   d. generational segmentation.

4. Defining a target market based on their gender is an example of:
   a. demographic segmentation.
   b. psychographic segmentation.
   c. life stage segmentation.
   d. generational segmentation.

5. Defining a target market based on their passion to work out is an example of:
   a. demographic segmentation.
   b. psychographic segmentation.
   c. life stage segmentation.
   d. generational segmentation.

 # Apply…

1. In groups, consider the following: You are the marketing manager of the Faraday Future FF91, an electric vehicle that can go 0–60 mph in 2.39 seconds (https://www.ff.com/us/). What problem does your product solve? Who is your target audience and how do you reach them? What would the profile of this client possibly look like?

_____

_____

_____

_____

_____

_____

_____

_____

_____

_____

_____

_____

_____

_____

_____

_____

_____

_____

_____

_____

_____

_____

_____

_____

_____

_____

_____

_____

_____

_____

_____

_____

to be continued

Apply...

continued

2. In groups, consider the following: The Toronto Blue Jays have had a successful run at the World Series championship over the past couple of years. Tickets sales have been strong during that time but lately, the team's performance has been less than stellar and fans are not frequenting the ballpark as they used to. As the marketing manager of the blue jays, you decide to take on a marketing strategy to bring the fans back to the ballpark. Who do you believe would be the ideal target audience? Would you segment based on demographic, psychographic segmentation, life stage segmentation, or generational factors? Hint . . . here are some sites to help you develop that profile: https://tinyurl.com/flextext-jays-attendance and https://tinyurl.com/flextext-jays-lists.

KNOW...

Learning Objectives

1. Know Porters Five Forces model and why it is important in setting out and building strategy The Five Forces model is a reality check which helps marketers to assess the attractiveness and influencers of the market and the opportunity for the business to succeed. The weaker these five forces are, the greater the opportunity will be for a brand or company to succeed. Vice versa, the stronger these forces are, the more difficult it will be to perform effectively and to get the best results from the market.

2. Marketing management's objective is to design strategies that will build strong and profitable relationships with consumers. Larger and faster growing segments may not always be the most appealing to market. They may require too much effort and time, may not be profitable, and may require added resources. Therefore, again, the marketer has to be mindful of the business objectives and what they have set out to accomplish.

3. A target market is the customer or organization that will ultimately buy a company's products or services. As a marketer, the target market is the person that you will design products and marketing programs for. What it entails, is the use of your advertising dollars and brand promotion ventures to capture the attention and interest of those who are definitely interested in what you have to offer. Marketing your product to a specific audience is a more affordable and effective method of reaching potential clientele and generating business.

4. A target market: *"a set of buyers sharing common needs or characteristics that the company decides to serve".*

5. There are four different strategies used to segment a market: undifferentiated, differentiated, niche, and micromarketing. An *undifferentiated* or *mass marketing* strategy and focus on the common needs of the whole market rather than on what is different of its consumers. A *differentiated strategy* divides a large target audience into smaller sets of consumers with common wants, needs, and interests. A *niche strategy* allows you to place all your marketing efforts on a small but specific and well-defined segment of the population and finally, a *micromarketing strategy allows* you to tailor products and marketing efforts to suit the tastes of a small and specific group.

6. Which market targeting strategy is chosen depends on many factors. None of the strategies above works best in every situation. Rather, the market targeting strategy depends on several characteristics of the company. When choosing a market targeting strategy, the company should consider the company's resources, the degree of product variability, the product life cycle, the market variability, and the competitors' marketing strategies.

7. A marketer can define a target market in several different ways. Target market customers can be defined by the type of business they serve, their geography, their demography, their psychography, their generation, their life stage, or their behavioural use of the product or service.

- **Consumer or Business**
  - ◊ Is your customer a B2B (business-to-business) or B2C (business-to-consumer)?

- **Geographic**
  - ◊ Where do they live, work, vacation, or do business?

- **Demographic**
  - ◊ What is their gender, age, income level, education level, and marital status?

- **Psychographic**
  - ◊ What are their internal attitudes and values?

- **Generation**
  - ◊ What generation were they born in—Baby Boomers, Gen X, or Gen Y?

- **Life stage**
  - ◊ What stage of life are they in? Post-college, retirement, newly married, newly divorced, or parenting young children?

- **Behavioural**
  - ◊ How often do they use your product or a similar product?

Key Terms

Differentiated Strategy: Divides a large target audience into smaller sets of consumers with common wants, needs, and interests.

Micromarketing Strategy: Allows you to tailor products and marketing efforts to suit the tastes of a small and specific group.

Niche Strategy: Allows you to place all your marketing efforts on a small but specific and well-defined segment of the population.

Target Market: Consumers with common needs or characteristics that the company decides to serve.

Target Market Analysis: A systematic and comprehensive assessment that allows you to identify important characteristics about your target market and group them into categories based on those characteristics.

Undifferentiated or Mass Marketing: Strategy focuses on the common needs of the whole market rather than on what is different of its consumers.

Answers to Practice

Evaluating if the Market Segment Is a Good Fit
1. b   2. a   3. d   4. a   5. b

Selecting Target Market Segments
1. b   2. c   3. d   4. d   5. b

Selecting Target Market Segments
1. c   2. b   3. a   4. b   5. a

Choosing a Targeting Strategy
1. a   2. c   3. c   4. a   5. b

References

Armstrong, Gary; Kotler, Philip, Marketing: An Introduction, 13th Ed., ©2017. Reprinted and Electronically reproduced by permission of Pearson Education, Inc., New York, NY.

Kotler, A., Buchwitz, T. (2017). *Marketing: An Introduction*, Pearson Canada; p. 253.

Porter, M. (March-April, 1979). How competitive forces shape strategy. *Harvard Business Review, 57,* 86–89.

7 Positioning

LEARNING OBJECTIVES

LO1 Define positioning

LO2 Know what a positioning strategy is and why it is important in marketing

LO3 Understand how to use the positioning matrix

LO4 Learn how to develop a positioning statement

LO5 Describe the six different types of positioning strategies

LEARN...

A study conducted by the marketing research firm Yankelovich estimated that the average consumer sees somewhere close to 5,000 marketing messages daily. (Johnson, 2006)

Furthermore, a 2017 Ad Week study forecasted that the average person will spend more than 5 years of their lives on social media. (Cohen, 2017)

Add to these statistics avoidance options like remote controls, PVRs, online and mobile apps, and many direct streaming options to choose from and it is quite obvious that today's marketers have a daunting task when disseminating a message.

Of course most people will not be able to recall most of the messages they see but the basic business takeaway is that consumers, though involved, are over-communicated with by marketers who are vying for their time and attention. They are bombarded with commercials on their screens, in print ads, on brand labels, on their Facebook and Google Ad pages, their emails, mobile messages, and any other medium that can get their attention and compel them to buy.

If marketers want their message to carry meaning and connect with consumers, they have to decide upon a strategy that enables them to:

- identify the market segment they want to enter;
- select a target audience segment; and
- take on a position it want to occupy in those segments.

Positioning, the third and final part of the segmentation, targeting, and positioning (STP) process is marketing strategy that is designed to "filter the noise" and create an emotional bond between the consumer and the brand.

A product's position is the place the product occupies in consumer's minds relative to the competition. Positioning statements like "We try harder" for Avis,

"The ultimate driving machine" for BMW, and "Think different" by Apple, are examples of how marketers have used positioning to not only differentiate their brand but also change the way consumers perceive them.

The following chapter will highlight the importance of positioning in marketing and some of the strategies that marketers use to position their offers to consumers.

What Is Positioning and Why Is It Necessary?

LO1 Define positioning

After segmenting a market and then targeting a consumer, marketers should proceed to position a product within that market. This process is also known as the STP process (Figure 1).

The term *positioning* was first introduced in 1969 by Jack Trout. The concept was later popularized when Trout and his co-author Al Ries published a bestselling book under the title, *Positioning–The Battle for Your Mind,* in 1981. In their book, Trout and Ries argue that there is too much clutter and noise in the market-place and what should matter most to marketers is how to manipulate the mind of the consumer so that you can get them to place or "position" your brand first rather than the brand of your competition.

According to Ries and Trout (2001),

> *Positioning is not what you do to a product. Positioning is what you do to the mind of a prospect. That is, you position or place the product in the mind of the prospect.*

Not only do you have to manipulate the mind of your consumer but Trout and Ries go on to say that in order for marketers' positioning to work, they have to be strategic in their positioning to consumers by communicating their message at the most appropriate time and under the right circumstances.

According to Armstrong et al. (2017), "**positioning**" is defined as:

> *the arranging for a product to occupy a clear, distinctive, and desirable place relative to competing products in the minds of consumers.*

Positioning and Unique Selling Proposition

Positioning is close to another current marketing concept called the **unique selling proposition (USP)**. Though similar, positioning *is based on audiences' perceptions*, while USP is based on the *existing attributes of the product or service*. USP tends to be more tied to the tangible features and benefits of a product or service, whereas positioning is much closer to branding.

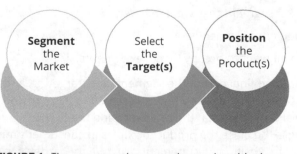

FIGURE 1 The segmentation, targeting, and positioning (STP) process.

Practice...

1. The term positioning was first coined by:
    a. David Ogilvy.
    b. Jack Trout.
    c. Philip Kotler.
    d. Don Draper.

2. STP stands for:
    a. Sales, targeting, prospects.
    b. Service, targeting, pitching.
    c. Segmentation, targeting, positioning.
    d. Situation, targeting, perception.

3. Trout and Ries argue that:
    a. consumers don't have enough product choice.
    b. the market is not as busy as it used to be.
    c. the market is undersaturated with choices.
    d. you need to manipulate the mind of your consumer.

4. Trout and Ries argue that:
    a. time and place are just as important as manipulating the consumer's mind.
    b. in order for positioning to work, your competitor's brand has to be positioned in the mind of the consumer first. This allows room for comparison.
    c. it's just as important to reach out to role models and influencers as it is to manipulate the consumer's mind.
    d. positioning is what you do to a product, not the mind of a prospect.

5. What makes positioning different than USP is that:
    a. it's based on the advertiser's perceptions of your brand.
    b. it's based on audience's perceptions of your brand.
    c. it's based on the existing attributes of the product or service.
    d. it's based on unique selling features of your product or service.

Apply...

1. Individually, pick your three top brand of jeans. List the brands in order of most favourite to least favourite. List two or three attributes that influenced your ranking (positioning). Be ready to share these with the class.

_____

_____

_____

_____

_____

_____

_____

_____

_____

_____

_____

_____

_____

_____

2. Individually, go online choosing a couple of your favourite products/brands, what do you think their USP is? Why do you think that way? Need a little more help in understanding what a USP is? Go to the following web site: https://tinyurl.com/flextext-usp

_____

_____

_____

_____

_____

_____

_____

_____

_____

_____

_____

_____

_____

_____

Positioning Strategy

L02 Know what a positioning strategy is and why it is important in marketing

What key words come to your mind when you think about companies such as Molson Canadian, Budweiser, and Corona? All are beer brands but position themselves on the basis of lifestyle. They can probably satisfy most beer drinkers' thirst and taste buds but are positioned in the minds of consumers differently. These industry leaders have developed positioning strategies that differentiate their brands and make Molson "the Canadian" beer drinker's beer; Budweiser the "king of beers"; and Corona the "vacationer's" beer.

A positioning strategy is an organized attempt for a brand to set itself apart from the crowd and influence the way their target audience perceives them. According to Ries and Trout (2001):

> Today's marketplace is no longer responsive to the strategies that worked in the past. There are just too many products, too many companies, and too much marketing noise.

Marketers research their product and try to find the words, symbols, or characteristics of their brand, product, or service that make them different and distinct from other category brands. It is believed that these differences are what holds a unique space within the minds of the target audience.

An effective **positioning strategy** focuses on some key areas that will allow it to compete and differentiate itself in the market:

- The strengths and weaknesses of the organization
- The needs of the customers and the market
- The position of competitors

Why Is Positioning Necessary?

- It's an opportunity for brands to *differentiate themselves and cut through the marketing clutter*.
- It allows the marketer to occupy *the consumer's mindset first and to assess the competing forces that are vying for the consumer's attention*.

Positioning allows marketers the opportunity to research the consumer and then paint a differentiating perception of a brand, product, service, or even business category.

Many well-positioned brands are disturbers of the peace because they have been able to differentiate themselves and develop strategies that create an emotional bond between their brand and their consumer. Examples of top of mind Canadian brands with exceptional and differentiating positioning strategies include lululemon and West Jet.

When most Canadians (and non-Canadians) think of the lululemon brand they see more than just a yoga and athletic clothing retailer. The brand has distinguished itself from other major athletic leisure or "athleisure" brands like Nike, Adidas, and Under Armour by selling high-quality products that are not only conducive to a healthy lifestyle but also "self-improvement, spirituality, self-discovery, holistic health, and global empathy". (Kolm, 2016)

West Jet has also made an impact on the minds and wallets of Canadians. When it first launched, the airline tried to differentiate itself from other "more serious and traditional" Canadian airline brands, by positioning itself to consumers as a fun, quirky, and alternative Canadian airline. These days the brand has added a *caring and down to earth tone* to their existing fun and quirky brand positioning. WestJet employees are also owners of the company (through the company's revenue sharing program) and the more recent marketing campaigns demonstrate how employees go beyond the efforts of other airlines to put a smile on their customers' faces. (Haynes, 2016)

Both these brands have become category leaders and have differentiated themselves among competitors. They have also managed to take a firm category position in the Canadian consumer's mindset.

The purpose of a positioning strategy is that it allows a company to spotlight on the specific areas where they can outshine and beat their competition.

For example, the Chipotle restaurant chain positions itself as a different kind of fast food chain. They offered something their fast food competitors did not offer and addressed the needs of customers who were looking for a bit more than hamburgers and French fries. Their *"Food With Integrity"* positioning sets them apart from other fast food competitors. They offer fresh and unprocessed ingredients, align themselves with smaller farms, and condemn agri-business. Spearheaded by their marketing, this positioning flows through every aspect of their business and they have managed to change the public's perception of the fast food business.

Source: Ken Wolter/Shutterstock

Practice...

1. A positioning strategy is:
    a. an organized attempt for two brands to come together.
    b. an organized attempt for a brand to position itself off the market.
    c. an organized attempt for a brand to set itself apart from the crowd.
    d. an organized attempt for a brand to compare itself to other brands.

2. Positioning strategies are necessary because:
    a. there is too much clutter in the market.
    b. consumers don't have enough choice.
    c. consumers cannot process the information that is presented to them.
    d. they allow parity with other brands in the market.

3. *At Avis, we are #2 so we try harder* . . . is an example of a:
    a. unique selling proposition.
    b. positioning statement.
    c. a business segment.
    d. consumer response.

4. A good positioning strategy should focus on:
    a. using strong imagery.
    b. the needs of the customer and the market.
    c. the needs of the organization.
    d. the needs of the advertising agency.

5. West Jet Airlines has developed a market positioning that is based on:
    a. low price trips and excursions.
    b. no hassle check-ins.
    c. exceptional customer service that goes beyond the flight.
    d. exceptional lounge and rest areas.

 **Apply...**

1. Individually, consider the following: Remember—an effective positioning strategy focuses on some key areas that will allow it to compete and differentiate itself in the market:

   - The strengths and weaknesses of the organization
   - The needs of the customers and the market
   - The position of competitors

   What do you think the positioning strategy is for Amazon (https://www.amazon.com/)? Use the three bullets listed above to help you develop your response.

   _____

   _____

   _____

   _____

   _____

   _____

   _____

   _____

   _____

   _____

   _____

   _____

2. In groups of up to four people, go to Canada Goose's web site and (http://www.canadagoose.com/ca/en/home-page) try to figure out what the positioning strategy is for Canada Goose. Review what you feel is their strengths and weaknesses, the view they have of customer's needs, and how their competitors are positioned.

   How does Canada Goose move through the clutter?

   _____

   _____

   _____

   _____

   _____

   _____

   _____

   _____

   _____

Positioning Strategy—The Positioning Matrix

L03 Understand how to use the positioning matrix

In advertising, the first product to establish the position, has an enormous advantage ... its best to have the best product in your field, but it's even better to be the first. (Ries & Trout, 2001)

The term "positioning" refers to the consumer's perception of a product or service in relation to its competitors. Marketers need to ask:

- *what is the position of the product that they are marketing, in the mind of the consumer?*

- *how do potential buyers see the product?*

Products and/or services are mapped together on a **"positioning matrix"**, which allows the marketer a chance to compare his/her product to that of other competitors. It's important to note that the exercise is all about individual "perception". Though there will be similarities, perception differs from person to person and, therefore, the exact positioning of a product or service will not be exactly the same but different from person to person.

Positioning Matrix Steps

- The marketer draws out the map and decides upon a variable for each axis (Figures 2 and 3).

  ◊ These variables can be anything but should be pertinent to your product and line of business.

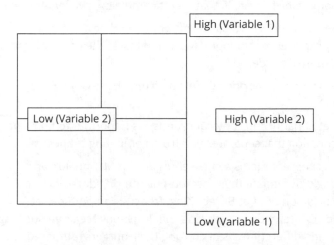

FIGURE 2 The positioning matrix template.

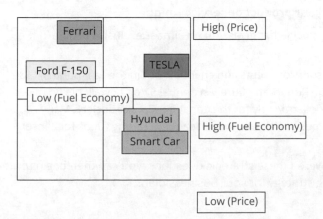

FIGURE 3 Positioning matrix example (Tesla automobiles).

- The individual products are then mapped out on the matrix.
  - ◊ Any gaps could be regarded as possible areas for new products.

Once mapped, the marketer will decide upon a competitive position which will enable them to distinguish their own products from the offerings of their competition.

Communication Tools (2009) suggest completing the exercise by answering the following six questions:

1. What position do you currently own?

2. What position do you want to own?

3. Whom you have to defeat to own the position you want?

4. Do you have the resources to do it?

5. Can you persist until you get there?

6. Are your tactics supporting the positioning objective you set?

A company's positioning strategy is affected by a number of variables related to customers' motivations and requirements, as well as by its competitors' actions. But how do you differentiate your product or service from that of your competitors and then position it to you target market? The following are some other strategic questions a marketer can ask when developing a positioning strategy:

- **What is your customer really buying from you?**
  - ◊ Is there something intangible that might come along with your brand?
  - ◊ Remember. Starbucks isn't just selling coffee and beverages, it sells a consistent experience that looks, feels, and tastes the same, no matter when or where it's ordered.

- **How is your product or service different from those of your competitors?**
  - ◊ In a market of parity and copy-cat brands, it's important to find a point of differentiation that separates you from competing brands.
  - ◊ To most, a cheeseburger is a cheeseburger. But McDonald's and Burger King differentiate their fast food by offering different side dishes (onion rings at Burger King, french-fried potatoes at McDonald's), different toys with kids' meals (Happy Meals versus King Jr. meals), and different ways of cooking their burgers (Burger King's are broiled and McDonald's, grilled).

- **What makes your product or service unique?**
  - ◊ What is so special that gives you an almost exclusive profile in the market?
  - ◊ Most bank sponsor events and charities. But in the Fall months, CIBC sponsors the Run for the Cure. An annual 5k or 1k walk or run raises millions of dollars yearly for the Canadian Cancer Society. Many consumers position the bank as a leader in raising funds for cancer research.

Once you've answered these strategic questions, you can then begin to develop a positioning strategy for your business plan.

Practice...

1. A "positioning matrix":
   a. allows marketers a chance to compare their product to that of other competitors.
   b. allows marketers a chance to match their product to that of other competitors.
   c. positions the highest sellers of product in each category.
   d. is not about perception.

2. A positioning matrix is premised on:
   a. the consumer's perception of the brand.
   b. the competition's perception of the brand.
   c. the media's perception of the brand.
   d. the organization's perception of the brand.

3. Which automobile would hold the position of lowest priced energy efficient automobiles in the market?
   a. Cadillac Escalade
   b. Hummer
   c. Toyota Prius
   d. Ford F-150 pickup truck

4. Home Hardware has differentiated itself among other hardware stores by positioning itself as:
   a. a big box choice.
   b. the hardware store choice for small town Canadians.
   c. a cheaper priced hardware store choice for Canadians.
   d. a luxury hardware store retailer.

5. In order to have an effective positioning matrix, you need:
   a. four variables—two high and two low.
   b. two variables—one high and one low.
   c. one variable.
   d. no variables.

 **Apply...**

1. In groups of up to four, create a positioning matrix for one of the following companies:

   • Sephora
   • Sport Chek
   • Apple—iPhone
   • Designer Shoe Warehouse
   • Home Depot
   • Walmart

   Chose three or four competitors and place them on the grid as well. Your horizontal grid should be based on price of the product while your vertical grid should be labelled product quality.

   _____

   _____

   _____

   _____

   _____

   _____

   _____

   _____

   _____

   _____

   _____

   _____

   _____

   _____

   _____

   _____

   _____

   _____

   _____

   _____

   _____

   _____

   _____

   _____

   _____

to be continued

 **Apply...**

continued

2. In groups of up to four, answer the following:

Based on your matrix:

- What position is the company is?
- What position do you think they want to be in?
- Whom they have to compete with to be in the position they want?
- Are their marketing tactics supporting the positioning objective you believe they wish to be in?

Present your matrix and new positioning to the class.

Types of Positioning Strategies

 LO4 Learn how to develop a positioning statement

LO5 Describe the six different types of positioning strategies

> *In the communications jungle out there, the only hope is to score big, to be selective, to concentrate on narrow targets, to practice segmentation, in other words 'positioning'.* (Ries & Trout, 2001)

The positioning matrix allows the marketer to see the benefits a customer will receive from the product and to differentiate it from the competition. This is formalized in a positioning statement, which articulates how the product serves the customer in a way that the competition cannot or does not.

A **positioning statement** is an expression or summary of how a given product, service, or brand will fill a particular consumer need in a way that its competitors don't. In his book, *Crossing the Chasm*, Geoffrey Moore (1991) offers the following template for a positioning statement:

> *For (target customer) who (statement of the need or opportunity), the (product name) is a (product category) that (statement of key benefit—that is, compelling reason to buy).*

Based on your statement, an effective positioning strategy can be developed. Positioning strategy considers the strengths and weaknesses of the organization, the needs of the customers and market, and the position of competitors. The purpose of a positioning strategy is that it allows a company to spotlight their competitive advantage over their competition.

Competitive advantage is defined as *"an advantage over competitors gained by offering greater customer value, either through lower prices or by providing more benefits that justify higher prices."* (Armstrong et al., 2017)

Some of the more popular positioning strategies that a company can take on are: *cost, quality, flexibility, speed, innovation, and service.*

Cost Positioning Strategy

A **cost positioning strategy** focuses on ways to eliminate any wasteful procedures within the company and pass the savings on to their customers. Companies that follow this strategy, focus on ways to eliminate any wasteful procedures within the company and pass the savings on to their customers. They are a lower priced option in the market and though they are not known for excellent customer service they offer lower prices to their customers.

Retailers, like Dollarama, Food Basics, and No Frills, have aligned their operations to embrace a cost positioning strategy, to the point where they have become some of Canada's most recognizable and most popular brands.

Quality Positioning Strategy

Most companies worry about quality in a reactionary way by chasing after problems and defects. This can destroy a company's credibility in the marketplace by alienating customers and suppliers. Some smart companies choose to focus on a **quality positioning strategy** as a way of differentiating themselves from their competitors by focusing on exceptional features, performance, style, and/or design.

An example of a company utilizing a quality positioning strategy is Canada Goose. They have a strong global reputation for making extreme weather parkas that perform in the cold, are durable, have an elegant design, and come with a highly recognizable arm patch. The results are a loyal fan base ready to drop hundreds of dollars—and sometimes over $1,000—on a Canadian made winter coat that keeps them snug and warm.

Flexibility Positioning Strategy

Consumers embrace companies that are able to change products and services based on their needs. A **flexibility positioning strategy** is another way for companies to differentiate themselves from their competition by being able to produce a wide variety of products, introduce new products or modify old products quickly, and respond to customer needs immediately.

Mountain Equipment Co-op (MEC) is a strong example of a company that employs a flexibility positioning strategy. They were once known as a co-operative store that only sold climbing and back country equipment. Today they have evolved to embrace young urbanites of the millennial generation by adding more accessible outdoor activity lines for cycling, running, and yoga gear to its traditional offering. Their strategy has paid off by being recognized as Canada's Top brand in 2016 and 2017 by Canadian Business magazine. (Philp, 2016)

Speed Positioning Strategy

Another source of competitive advantage for companies is to use a **speed positioning strategy**. Fast food and delivery companies are natural fits for a speed positioning strategy and compete on delivering their products and services quickly to their customers. This strategy is not exclusive to the food and delivery service industry. Many companies establish sophisticated logistical operations to offer immediate delivery of the products in order to beat their competition. The latest trend is for companies like Amazon to develop drones that they hope to use to deliver orders to customers within hours, once air traffic regulations allow it.

Companies like Hakim Optical take pride on having operations in 140 stores across Canada that allow 1 hour delivery of eyeglasses.

Innovation Positioning Strategy

Companies like Tesla, Facebook, Uber, Netflix, Google, and Amazon have remained industry leaders in providing the marketplace with exciting new and innovative products and have adopted an **innovation positioning strategy** in their marketing.

These companies offer a constant flow of leading edge, advanced products to consumers for a fair price and spend enormous amounts of money on hiring the best talent to design innovative products that appeal to consumers. Consumers tend to spend a hefty amount with these innovative brands just so they can lay claim to owning the latest and greatest in communicative technology.

Service Positioning Strategy

Companies can also select a **service positioning strategy** in order to differentiate themselves from others by providing superior customer service.

In the crowded Canadian retail landscape, new entrant Nordstrom is a brand that has raised the service bar. Nordstrom goes above and beyond in a way that customers never forget. They have a no questions asked return policy, offer "shoe tying lessons" for kids, and go above and beyond in a way that most customers never forget.

> *Everything is done with the customer in mind. If it doesn't benefit the customer, it's not customer service . . . Everybody has a Nordstrom*

story . . . floor staff cheerfully accepting unabashedly damaged returns, no questions asked; Nordstrom employees helping mall shoppers carry purchases from other stores to their cars; and an often-repeated tale about a customer in Anchorage, Alaska, who returned a set of tires to a Nordstrom location—despite the fact that the chain doesn't actually sell tires. (Toller, 2015)

Practice...

1. A company that uses a cost positioning strategy:
   a. focuses on ways to eliminate any wasteful procedures within the company and pass the savings on to their customers.
   b. focuses on being able to produce a wide variety of products, introduce new products or modify old products quickly, and respond to customer needs.
   c. focuses on ways of differentiating themselves from their competitors by focusing on exceptional features, performance, style, and/or design.
   d. focuses on delivering their products and services quickly to their customers.

2. A company that uses a *quality positioning strategy*:
   a. focuses on ways to eliminate any wasteful procedures within the company and pass the savings on to their customers.
   b. focuses on being able to produce a wide variety of products, introduce new products or modify old products quickly, and respond to customer needs.
   c. focuses on ways of differentiating themselves from their competitors by focusing on exceptional features, performance, style, and/or design.
   d. focuses on delivering their products and services quickly to their customers.

3. A company that uses a *flexibility positioning strategy*:
   a. focuses on being able to produce a wide variety of products, introduce new products or modify old products quickly, and respond to customer needs.
   b. focuses on ways of differentiating themselves from their competitors by focusing on exceptional features, performance, style, and/or design.

   c. focuses on delivering their products and services quickly to their customers.
   d. focuses on being able to produce a wide variety of products, introduce new products or modify old products quickly, and respond to customer needs

4. A company that uses a *speed positioning strategy*:
   a. focuses on being able to produce a wide variety of products, introduce new products or modify old products quickly, and respond to customer needs.
   b. focuses on ways of differentiating themselves from their competitors by focusing on exceptional features, performance, style, and/or design.
   c. focuses on delivering their products and services quickly to their customers.
   d. focuses on being able to produce a wide variety of products, introduce new products or modify old products quickly, and respond to customer needs.

5. A company that uses an *innovation positioning strategy*:
   a. focuses on offering a constant flow of leading edge, advanced products to consumers for a fair price answer choice.
   b. focuses on being able to produce a wide variety of products, introduce new products or modify old products quickly, and respond to customer needs.
   c. focuses on ways of differentiating themselves from their competitors by focusing on exceptional features, performance, style, and/or design.
   d. focuses on being able to produce a wide variety of products, introduce new products or modify old products quickly, and respond to customer needs.

Apply...

1. Write about two fast food companies (that is, Subway, Burger King, Pizza Hut, Wendy's) that utilize a *speed positioning strategy*. Provide examples of their marketing and demonstrate where the speed positioning strategy was used. Using Moore's template for positioning, create a positioning statement for each company, and present it to class.

   • *Moore's template*

   "For (*target customer*) who (*statement of the need or opportunity*), the (*product name*) is a (*product category*) that (*statement of key benefit—that is, compelling reason to buy*)".

to be continued

Apply...

continued

2. Write about two technology companies (that is, Samsung, Sony, Apple, Microsoft, Dell) that utilize an *innovation positioning strategy*. Provide examples of their marketing and demonstrate where the speed positioning strategy was used. Using Moore's template for positioning, create a positioning statement for each company, and present it to class.

    • *Moore's template*

    "For (*target customer*) who (*statement of the need or opportunity*), the (*product name*) is a (*product category*) that (*statement of key benefit—that is, compelling reason to buy*)".

    _____

    _____

    _____

    _____

    _____

    _____

    _____

    _____

    _____

    _____

    _____

    _____

    _____

    _____

    _____

    _____

    _____

    _____

    _____

    _____

    _____

    _____

    _____

    _____

    _____

    _____

KNOW...

Learning Objectives

1. The term *positioning* was first introduced in 1969 by Jack Trout. The concept was later popularized when Trout and his co-author Al Ries published a bestselling book under the title, *Positioning—The Battle for Your Mind,* in 1981. Trout and Ries argue that the consumers are inundated with communications messages. Rather than force messages onto consumers, they argue that it is more important to be the first to place or "position" your brand, product, or service in the mind of the consumer first, before the competition. Positioning is the third step in the segmentation, targeting, and positioning (STP) process and should not be mistaken with the unique selling proposition (USP).

2. A *positioning strategy* is when a company chooses one or two important key areas to concentrate on and excels in those areas. The purpose of a positioning strategy is that it allows a company to spotlight specific areas where they can outshine and beat their competition. A firm's positioning strategy focuses on how it will compete in the market. An effective positioning strategy considers the strengths and weaknesses of the organization, the needs of the customers and market, and the position of competitors.

3. A "*positioning matrix*", allows the marketer a chance to compare (in a matrix) their product's position in comparison to competitors and how potential buyers see the product. The matrix is an individual perception of how the brand is perceived in the mind of the consumer and measures four variables (high to low) variables. Depending on where your brand, product, or service maps on the matrix, you can then decide on what type of strategy to take on.

4. A *positioning statement*, articulates how the product serves the customer in a way that the competition cannot or does not. A *positioning statement* is an expression or summary of how a given product, service, or brand will fill a particular consumer need in a way that its competitors don't. The template developed by Moore, *"For (target customer) who (statement of the need or opportunity), the (product name) is a (product category) that (statement of key benefit—that is, compelling reason to buy).* Once the positioning statement has been developed and tested, a strategy can be developed.

5. Some of the more popular positioning strategies that a company can take on are: cost, quality, flexibility, speed, innovation, and service.

Key Terms

Competitive Advantage: This is defined as "an advantage over competitors gained by offering greater customer value, either through lower prices or by providing more benefits that justify higher prices."

Cost Positioning Strategy: A positioning strategy taken on by a company that focuses on ways to eliminate any wasteful procedures within the company and pass the savings on to their customers.

Flexibility Positioning Strategy: A positioning strategy taken on by a company to differentiate themselves from their competition by being able to produce a wide variety of products, introduce new products or modify old products quickly, and respond to customer needs immediately.

Innovation Positioning Strategy: A positioning strategy taken on by a company to differentiate themselves from their competition by focusing on their ability to provide the marketplace with exciting new and innovative products.

Positioning: The approach and efforts that marketers take to clearly and distinctly arrange and prioritize their products in the minds of consumers versus their competition.

Positioning Matrix: A positioning matrix allows the marketer a chance to "map" or compare his/her product to that of other competitors.

Positioning Statement: An expression or summary of how a given product, service or brand will fill a particular consumer need in a way that its competitors don't. Geoffrey Moore created a positioning statement template to assist marketers: *"For (target customer) who (statement of the need or opportunity), the (product name) is a (product category) that (statement of key benefit—that is, compelling reason to buy). Unlike (primary competitive alternative), our product (statement of primary differentiation)."*

Positioning Strategy: Focuses on the strengths and weaknesses of the organization, the needs of the customers and the market, and the position of competitors. These key areas will allow the brand to compete and differentiate itself in the market. The purpose of a positioning strategy is that it allows a company to spotlight on the specific areas where they can outshine and beat their competition.

Quality Positioning Strategy: A positioning strategy taken on by a company that focuses on differentiating themselves from their competitors by focusing on exceptional features, performance, style, and/or design.

Service Positioning Strategy: A positioning strategy taken on by a company to differentiate themselves from their competition by focusing on their superior customer service.

Speed Positioning Strategy: A positioning strategy taken on by a company which differentiates them from the competition by focusing on their ability to deliver their products and services quickly to their customers.

USP: Unique Selling Proposition, the tangible features and benefits of a product or service that a marketer promotes. Positioning is more tied to the "mind" of the consumer.

Answers to Practice

What Is Positioning and Why Is It Necessary?
1. b   2. c   3. d   4. a   5. b

Positioning Strategy
1. c   2. a   3. b   4. b   5. c

Positioning Strategy—The Positioning Matrix
1. a   2. a   3. c   4. b   5. a

Types of Positioning Strategies
1. a   2. c   3. d   4. c   5. a

References

Al Ries, Jack Trout, Positioning, The Battle for Your Mind, McGraw Hill, 2001.

Armstrong, Gary; Kotler, Philip, Marketing: An Introduction, 13th Ed., ©2017. Reprinted and Electronically reproduced by permission of Pearson Education, Inc., New York, NY.

Armstrong, Kotler, Trifts, Buchwitz. (2018). *Marketing, An Introduction*. Pearson.

Canadian Business Magazine, How Nordstrom built the world's best customer-service machine. Carol Toller, March 5, 2015, http://www.canadianbusiness.com/innovation/secrets-of-nordstrom-customer-service/

Communication Tools: Positioning and position mapping, January, 2009, https://www.odi.org/publications/5887-positioning-trout-ries

David, C. (March 22, 2017). How much time will the average person spend on social media during their life? *Ad Week*.

Geoffrey Moore, Crossing the Chasm, p.114, Harper Collins Publishers, 1991.

Haynes, M. (February, 2016). Inside West Jet's fight for the skies. Strategy Magazine. Retrieved from http://strategyonline.ca/2016/02/26/inside-westjets-fight-for-the-skies/.

Johnson, C. (September 14, 2006). Cutting through the clutter. *CBS*.

Kolm, J. (May, 2016). Lululemon shifts its perspective for first global campaign. *Strategy Magazine*. Retrieved from http://strategyonline.ca/2017/05/16/lululemon-shifts-its-approach-for-first-global-campaign/.

Philp, B. (October 11, 2016). Canada's best brands 2017: The top 25. *Canadian Business Magazine.* Retrieved from http://www.canadianbusiness.com/lists-and-rankings/best-brands/canadas-best-brands-2017-the-top-25/image/26/.

8 Competitive Advantage

LEARNING OBJECTIVES

 LO1 Differentiate between "competitive" and "sustainable competitive" advantage

LO2 Understand the importance of a business mission statement and why it helps to identify a company's competitive advantage

 LO3 Understand the purpose and use of a SWOT analysis

LO4 Define and classify the four strategic alternatives used to grow and market a business

LEARN...

Since 1986, "It tastes awful and it works" has been the advertising slogan for Buckley's Mixture (Barone & DeCarlo, 2003).

Though the benefit of bad taste may not be one of the attributes that most brands use to promote their products, Buckley's has leveraged "awful taste" to the point where they have differentiated themselves from the competitive pack as one of the worst tasting cough and cold medicines in the market. In return, this strategic advantage has granted them a 10% market share of the cough and cold category in Canada.

Almost every company claims that their products and services can make you "jump higher", "last longer', and even "live longer" than others. Most successful brands stress their unique benefits and play up the things that they do better than anyone else. But why would consumers select your brand or want to do business with you rather than your competitors? What's the unique benefit or competitive advantage of selecting your brand over that of others? When you can answer this question, then you can determine and exploit your advantage, versus that of your competition, in all your marketing.

A competitive advantage is an advantage that is gained over the competition by offering customers greater value either through lower prices or by providing additional benefits and service that justify similar or possibly higher prices. Finding and nurturing an edge over your competition can mean increased profit, loyalty, and a brand—like Buckley's—that is sustainable and successful over a long period of time. It's important for marketers to reinforce this edge in all their communication and to articulate the benefit(s) that they provide to their target market that gives them an edge over the competition.

The following chapter will look at some of the different tools that marketers use to gain a sustainable competitive advantage over their competition.

Competitive Advantage: What Is it?

L01 Differentiate between "competitive" and "sustainable competitive" advantage

Competitive advantage is defined as:

> *The advantage over competitors gained by offering greater customer value, either through lower prices or by providing more benefits that justify higher prices.* (Armstrong et al., 2017)

Essentially a competitive advantage tells consumers why a company or brand believes that their products or services are better than that of the competition. For some companies, particularly those in markets where the products or services are less differentiated, finding an advantage can be difficult and hard to sustain, due to market changes and competitors that try to match your advantages. Having a competitive advantage requires researching and finding your competitive edge and why it's important to your customers. This then has to be followed by constant maintenance of your environment and finding ways to continuously sustain your edge, so that the competition either cannot or will take a long time to match (Barone & DeCarlo, 2003).

> *Building sustainable competitive advantages revolves around differentiating a product from the competition along attributes that are important and relevant to customers.*

To be successful, marketing needs to be able to articulate the *benefit the brand, product, or service provides the target market (or customers), which the competition can't.* This in essence will be the competitive advantage that you take to market and it is important to answer most of these questions (Amadeo, 2017).

Benefit

- What is the benefit your product provides and offers?
- Is the benefit something your customers *truly* need and that offers them *real* value?
- Are you aware of new trends that affect your product?

Target market

- Who are your current and potential customers?
- You've got to know exactly who buys from you, and how you can make their life better.
- How do your product's features and advantages benefit your customers?

Competition

- Which companies or brands are you in direct competition with?
- What products and services do they provide?
- What is their benefit to customers?
- What prevailing trends exist in the market?

What Is a Sustainable Competitive Advantage?

The last two words are what most people understand fairly readily, which (as described above), is the concept of having something that your competitors don't. What **sustainability** further addresses is how long you are able to maintain your edge and whether or not it's easy for your competition to erase your **competitive advantage** and how long will it take them to match it or catch up?

Michael Porter outlined cost leadership, differentiation, and focus as the three primary ways companies achieve a sustainable competitive advantage (Porter, 1998).

Cost Leadership: It means you provide reasonable value at a lower price. Examples of cost leader marketers include the Dollarama, No Frills supermarkets, and Walmart brands. All provide products at a reasonable value to their customers.

Differentiation: It means that you deliver better benefits to your customer than anyone else. Companies typically achieve differentiation with *innovation, quality, or customer service.*

- Innovation means that you meet the same needs in a new way.
  - ◊ An excellent example of this is Nespresso. The coffee pod company was innovative because it allowed you to make "café" type drinks in the comfort of your home at fractions of the café price.
- Quality means that you provide the best product or service.
  - ◊ Tiffany's can charge more because patrons see "their little blue box" as the epitome of fine jewellery—especially engagement rings and wedding bands
- Customer service means that going out of the way to delight shoppers.
  - ◊ Nordstrom's was the first to allow customer returns with no questions asked.

Focus means you understand and service your target market better than anyone else. You can use either cost leadership or differentiation to do that. One key to focus success is to choose one specific target market. Often it's a tiny niche that larger companies don't serve.

For example, credit unions like Meridian use a focus strategy to gain a sustainable competitive advantage. They target local small businesses and individuals in their immediate community and make them "member owners". This way their target audience enjoys the personal and local touch that big banks may not be able to give, as well as an opportunity to share a piece the credit union's profits.

Practice...

1. In a nutshell, competitive advantage is all about:
    a. being a competitive company.
    b. offering value to customers that is just as good as the competition.
    c. offering value to customers that is greater than that offered by the competition.
    d. having the technology to better compete against other companies.

2. A competitive advantage tells consumers why a company or brand:
    a. believes that their products or services are not as good as that of the competition.
    b. believes that their products or services are just as good as that of the competition.
    c. believes that their products or services are better than that of the competition.
    d. believes that their products or services are competitive with that of the competition.

3. Competitive advantage requires the marketer to articulate:
    a. to the target market the benefits that the competition can't offer.
    b. to the competition the benefits that the target can't offer.
    c. to the corporate stakeholders the advantages of the brand.
    d. to the target markets the benefits that the competition's products and services offer.

4. Being successfully sustainable, allows:
    a. the competition to quickly catch up to your advantages.
    b. you the marketer to maintain your edge over your competitors for a long period of time.
    c. easy access to your competitors to match your strengths.
    d. you the marketer the opportunity to match your competitors' strengths.

5. Porter outlined _____ as the three primary ways companies achieve a sustainable competitive advantage.
    a. strengths, weaknesses, and strengths
    b. cost leadership, differentiation, and focus
    c. benefit, target, and competition
    d. sustainability, targeting, and focus

Apply...

1. In group, consider the following: You are a member of the marketing team for Tesla (https://www.tesla.com/en_CA/), who has been assigned to develop the communication message for the next 12 months. Make sure to clearly identify in your messaging several key benefits that *your organization provides* to the target market (or customers), which the competition can't. Present your benefits to the class.

_____

_____

_____

_____

_____

_____

_____

_____

_____

_____

_____

2. In pairs, present your findings in next week's class.

   Recall the definition of cost leadership—means you provide reasonable value at a lower price. Come up with three companies that use cost leadership to achieve a sustainable advantage. Be able to provide supporting rationale for the business you picked.

   Recall the definition of differentiation—you deliver better benefits to your customer than anyone else. Companies typically achieve differentiation with *innovation, quality, or customer service.* Come up with three companies that use differentiation to achieve a sustainable advantage. Be able to provide supporting rationale for the business you picked.

_____

_____

_____

_____

_____

_____

_____

_____

_____

_____

How to Develop a Business Mission Statement

 Understand the importance of a business mission statement and why it helps to identify a company's competitive advantage

The foundation of any marketing plan is the firm's business **mission statement**. It is defined as *"a statement of the organization's purpose—what it wants to accomplish in the larger environment."* (Armstrong et al., 2017)

Beyond the definition, a mission statement explains why a company is in business, their point of differentiation, what they're trying to accomplish in the market, who they serve, and what type of experiences they expect to create for their customers.

Though it's a lot to say in just a few words, a good mission statement should motivate all parties involved with the brand (the organization, the marketer, and the consumers) and create an opportunity for them to better understand the nature of the business, their advantage, and reason to exist. They also allow the marketer with a foundation that helps to shape the tone and character of the brand and marketing campaigns that will follow.

When a company's mission focuses too closely on their products or services rather than the benefits (both immediate and enhanced) to their consumers, then the company is exhibiting marketing myopia. **Marketing myopia** is defined as:

> *The mistake of paying more attention to the specific products a company offers than to the benefits and experiences produced by these products.* (Armstrong et al., 2017)

It's easy to focus on a company's films, but a company like Walt Disney produces more than that. Their brand is also about resorts and creating experiences where families can immerse themselves in Disney's world of wonder. Walt Disney Resort's mission goes beyond the typical vacation resort experience by aiming to provide visitors with a destination that allows all of their dreams to come true.

Source: Spatuletail/Shutterstock.

Therefore, it is important for a company to look beyond the immediate gratification that their products and services bring to their customers when forming a mission.

A good example of a business mission statement is Pearson's, whose mission statement reads as follows:

To help people make progress in their lives through learning.

Source: Ververidis Vasilis/Shutterstock.

This statement covers a lot of ground, which allows Pearson to delve into all aspects of the Canadian educational market.

Practice...

1. A mission statement is:
   a. a company's account of earnings.
   b. a company's purpose.
   c. a company's forecast of the marketing initiatives it will undertake.
   d. another word for marketing plan.

2. A mission statement is important to the marketer because:
   a. it showcases the budget that the marketer has to execute a campaign.
   b. it sets the tone and character of the brand.
   c. it allows for marketing myopia to occur.
   d. it allows them to focus on the products and services that they will take to market.

3. When a company's mission statement focuses mostly on their products or services rather than the benefits, the company exhibits:
   a. a sustainable competitive advantage.
   b. a competitive advantage.
   c. a differentiation in the marketplace.
   d. marketing myopia.

4. A good mission statement should motivate:
   a. the organization, the marketer, and consumers.
   b. the competition and the organization.
   c. the competition and consumers.
   d. the organization, the marketer, and competition.

5. Marketers who are guilty of marketing myopia:
   a. focus solely on the company's profits.
   b. focus solely on the company's internal organization structure.
   c. focus on marketing the company's products and services.
   d. focus on the matching the offers of the competition.

 Apply...

1. Source the mission statement of one of your favourite brands. Do you think that the brand does a good job at presenting its purpose to you as a consumer? Do you think that your brand could do better? If so, reword the mission statement so that it better defines you the consumer.

_____

_____

_____

_____

_____

_____

_____

_____

_____

_____

_____

_____

2. Armstrong defines a mission statement as *"a statement of the organization's purpose—what it wants to accomplish in the larger environment."* WestJet's mission statement reads: "To enrich the lives of everyone in WestJet's world." In your opinion, how effective is this as a mission statement. What would you do to improve it? Present your new mission statement for Air Canada to the class. Click on this link to view their mission, values, and culture: https://tinyurl.com/flextext-westjet

_____

_____

_____

_____

_____

_____

_____

_____

_____

_____

_____

_____

_____

What Is SWOT: Situation Analysis in Marketing

 Understand the purpose and use of a SWOT analysis

Situational Analysis

Have you ever had to decide whether to take a risk? Maybe the risk was picking an apartment to rent or choosing your college or university?

When it comes to making a decision, most people and businesses make a list of the pros and cons to a choice, assess them, and then make a final decision. This decision-making process is called conducting a **SWOT analysis**, also known as a **situational analysis**.

After a mission statement has been created, marketers do not dive head first into creating a marketing plan or creating television ads, or social media sites. They first look at all internal and external resources and threats their business will face and conduct a situational or S.W.O.T. analysis (where S.W.O.T. stands for internal strengths, internal weaknesses, external opportunities and external threats). The SWOT helps marketers in two ways:

1. It helps to assess and understand the current and potential environment in which a business competes.

2. It helps to identify the competitive advantage it will use to differentiate itself to consumers and to face competitors in the marketplace.

To begin a basic SWOT analysis, create a four-cell grid or four lists, one for each SWOT component (Figure 1):

Strengths

What you do well?

What makes you stand out?

Your advantages over competitors

Weaknesses

Areas that are a struggle

What do your customers complain about?

Areas for improvement

Opportunities

Areas where your strengths are not being fully utilized

Emerging trends that fit with your company's strengths

Product/service areas that you could do well in but are not yet competing in

Threats

Potential problems or risks that could damage your business

Are your competitors becoming stronger?

Are there emerging trends that amplify one of your weaknesses?

FIGURE 1 SWOT matrix. Four-cell SWOT analysis grid highlighting the strengths, weaknesses, opportunities, and threats.

Internal Strengths and Weaknesses

The first part of the SWOT analysis is examining a company's internal strengths and weaknesses. In this step, a marketing manager looks internally at the company's resources, such as finances, engineering, marketing, employees, and production, to see where they excel or need improvement. Marketing managers should not just look at the current situation of the firm, but also look at past historical sales, profit, and cost data.

When looking for a company's strengths, it's important to ask:

- What you're best at?
- What you're known for?
- Do you have a unique selling proposition?
  ◦ A **USP,** or **unique selling proposition**, is something that you're very good at, but your competition is not.

Amazon would be an example of a company with great internal strengths in the area of human resources and employee development. They offer new employees an intensive, month-long training and leadership program prior to hire and prepay 95% of tuition for employees at fulfillment centers to take courses in in-demand fields (Thottam, n.d.).

When looking for company weaknesses, a marketing manager asks:

- What areas need improvement?
- What could our competitors view as a weakness?
- What issues could cost the company sales and/or profit?

They then attack those areas and have a plan in place to protect and improve their situation. If a company is realistic upfront, then they're less likely to fail down the road or to be caught by a competitor. A marketing manager needs to consider factors like poor location of the business, inexperienced marketing, poor quality, or poor reputation as a big weakness. Many marketing departments try to address their weaknesses in marketing campaigns.

An example of this would be Telus. The big three Canadian telecommunication companies rank low in customer service indices. In its "expect more" advertising campaign, Telus has tried to address its customer service weakness by telling customers that they always strive to be "the best mobile service provider today and will do even better than the best tomorrow". In fact, internally, it strives to be the world's most recommended company (Pellegrini, 2015).

External Opportunities and Threats

The second part of the SWOT analysis is examining the external opportunities and threats.

Marketing managers analyze the overall marketing environment. They can accomplish this difficult task through the use of **environmental scanning**. Environmental scanning assesses the economic, cultural, demographic, political, ecological, and technological conditions and changes that exist in the environment. Environmental scanning is done in order to see what changes are happening in the marketplace that could result in a positive opportunity or a negative threat.

Marketers can use the information to design new objectives and strategies or modify existing objectives and strategies. They can also use the information to consider opportunities in new markets, mergers, or even take over an area left by an ineffective competitor.

Threats come in the form of new competitors, pricing wars, new product innovation from a competitor, or government intervention in your industry, such as new or higher taxes.

The Hudson's Bay Company (HBC), one of the world's oldest businesses, has redefined its mission over and over in order to address both threats and opportunities in the market. It began primarily as a fur-trading company in 1670 and has outlived its retail rivals by changing with the times, often adopting threats as opportunities. HBC's portfolio today includes formats ranging from luxury to premium department stores to off-price fashion shopping destinations, with more than 480 stores and over 66,000 employees around the world. HBC's leading banners across North America and Europe include Hudson's Bay, Lord & Taylor, Saks Fifth Avenue, Gilt, Saks OFF 5TH, Galeria Kaufhof in Germany, and Galleria INNO in Belgium. It also has significant investments in real estate joint ventures with Simon Property Group Inc. in the United States and RioCan Real Estate Investment Trust in Canada (HBC.com).

Practice...

1. Why is it important for companies to use a SWOT analysis?
   a. It analyzes strengths, weaknesses, obligations, and threats.
   b. It analyzes strengths, weaknesses, opportunities, and threats.
   c. It analyzes strengths, weaknesses, opportunities, and time.
   d. It analyzes strong points, weak points, opportunities, and threats.

2. Why is environmental scanning used in marketing?
   a. To determine the feasibility and potential of a marketing strategy.
   b. To analyze the overall marketing environment, including economic, political, and technological changes.
   c. To determine how to market products specifically to a more eco-friendly audience.
   d. To determine what strengths a company has that can be used to positively affect the environment.

3. A marketing team just conducted a SWOT analysis of their new product. What should their next steps be?
   a. Make sure that weaknesses are offset by opportunities and threats are turned into strengths.
   b. Make sure that opportunities are offset by threats and strengths are turned into weaknesses.
   c. Make sure that weaknesses are offset by the strengths and threats are turned into opportunities.
   d. Make sure that strengths are offset by weaknesses and opportunities and turned into threats.

4. What is the USP of a company?
   a. It is a product that provides a company with a competitive advantage over their competition.
   b. It is something that a company is very good at, but their competition is not.
   c. It is something a company has that is the same as that of their competition.
   d. It is when a company has a margin of profitability higher than 25%.

5. The first steps management should consider in determining the feasibility of a new project or expansion project is to determine:
   a. external weaknesses and opportunities.
   b. internal strengths and weaknesses.
   c. external strengths and threats.
   d. internal opportunities and threats.

 Apply...

1. Dairy farmers in Canada (https://www.qualitymilk.ca/#header) for years have been trying to increase consumption of milk. Complete a SWOT analysis for this product, and develop a marketing campaign (12 months) to try to increase sales. Identify some of the communication mediums you would use. Why did you pick the ones you did?

    _____

    _____

    _____

    _____

    _____

    _____

    _____

    _____

    _____

    _____

    _____

    _____

    _____

    _____

    _____

    _____

    _____

    _____

    _____

    _____

    _____

    _____

    _____

    _____

    _____

    _____

    _____

    _____

to be continued

 **Apply...**

continued

2. Complete an environmental scan of an industry you are interested in. Recall that *Environmental scanning assesses (macro environmental forces) the economic, cultural, demographic, political, ecological, and technological conditions and changes that exist in the environment. Environmental scanning is done in order to see what changes are happening in the marketplace that could result in a positive opportunity or a negative threat.* Not sure what industry to choose? How about golf industry, cosmetic, automotive, or newspaper.

_____

_____

_____

_____

_____

_____

_____

_____

_____

_____

_____

_____

_____

_____

_____

_____

_____

_____

_____

_____

_____

_____

_____

_____

Types of Strategic Alternatives for Growth Opportunities

LO4 Define and classify the four strategic alternatives used to grow and market a business

Four Strategic Alternatives

Once the SWOT analysis is completed and the marketer has decided on the advantage they will use to compete in the marketplace, the company's marketer(s) need to identify, evaluate, and select the opportunities and strategies to market their product or service.

These various **strategic alternatives** are the game plan that a company will choose in order to grow their share of market and get the largest growth and profits with the lowest risk. One useful device for identifying growth opportunities is the product-market expansion grid. It is a portfolio planning tool for identifying growth opportunities in four different ways: market penetration, market development, product development, and diversification (Figure 2).

A company that decides to use a **market penetration strategy** would plan to increase profits by increasing market share among existing customers. No changes are made to products in this circumstance but the marketer aims to make more sales to current customers. It might add more stores in the current market areas or promotions to entice and encourage customers to stop by more often, stay longer, or buy more. Marketers in all categories use market penetration to attract more business from existing customers and to retain them. Four Seasons Resorts, for example, ran a special summer promotion package at its hotel in Milan which offered guests who rented a suite with 2 days' rental of a Ferrari California Cabrio. Starbucks has used a market

FIGURE 2 The Product-market expansion grid. A portfolio planning tool for identifying growth opportunities in four different ways: market penetration, market development, product development, and diversification.

Based on Kotler, A., Buchwitz, T. (2017). *Marketing, An Introduction.* Pearson.

penetration strategy by adding an evening menu in some markets which features wine, beers, and taps to attract its existing customers and boost business beyond the breakfast rush.

A company that uses a **market development strategy** concentrates on identifying and developing new markets and customers for their existing products and services. One key way of achieving this is to find new ways to use existing products. Arm & Hammer Baking Soda constantly finds new ways to bring in additional customers. Their promotional campaigns always indicate the many uses of the product beyond a baking soda, such as cleaning pesticides off fruit, brushing your teeth, baking, and deodorizing.

Another way companies can increase their new customer base is to target new demographic and geographic markets. Companies like McDonald's and Starbucks have had much of their growth overseas and are looking to gain even more customers in Eastern Europe and Asia.

Another strategic alternative is product development. In a **product development strategy**, companies create modified or new products to their existing markets. Some examples of this type of strategy would be Microsoft's Xbox gaming console, Pretzel M&M's candy, and Apple's iPad. Companies constantly look for ideas for new products.

The last strategy a company can consider is called **diversification**. This strategy has the most risk because it may involve new product development and a push into new markets and categories that may be beyond the company's forte and comfort zone.

It is a risky leap but McDonald's starting of McCafe is an excellent example of diversification. By starting McCafe, they offered new products that were not available in traditional McDonald's restaurants and attracted customers that may not have come to McDonald's for burgers and fries. An example of a company that tried to diversify beyond its means is Roots. In 2001, it attempted to move into the airline business but failed for a variety of reasons including the fact that consumers weren't able to equate the clothing retailer's brand and values to that of an airline. When a firm is able to be successful at this strategy, they can reap large market share and profits but it is important for companies to thoroughly research the new product development process and the new markets they are planning to enter and to see if there is an appetite for this endeavor.

Practice...

1. What is a strategic alternative?
   a. The *biggest challenge* for a company
   b. Another way of thinking about marketing
   c. The *game plan* for the company to grow profits and market share
   d. The *last recipe for success* for a company

2. What are the four different strategic alternatives?
   a. Stars, cash cows, problem children, and dogs
   b. Penetration, development, target market, and stars
   c. Market penetration, market development, product development, and diversification
   d. Market penetration, market development, target market, and market response

3. Companies that create modified or new products to their existing markets use a _____ strategic alternative.
   a. market penetration
   b. market development
   c. product development
   d. diversification

4. Companies that develop new markets and customers for their existing products and services use a _____ strategic alternative.
   a. market penetration
   b. market development
   c. product development
   d. diversification

5. Companies that push into new markets and categories use a _____ strategic alternative.
   a. market penetration
   b. market development
   c. product development
   d. diversification

Apply...

1. In groups, give examples of how Tim Horton's (http://www.timhortons.com/ca/en/index.php) product development strategy has helped fuel the tremendous growth of this organization over the past 10 years.

_____

_____

_____

_____

_____

_____

_____

_____

_____

_____

to be continued

 # Apply...

continued

2. In groups, give examples of how Nike has been successful with product diversification and has also failed with product diversification. You may have to do some research online to identify areas.

_____
_____
_____
_____
_____
_____
_____
_____
_____
_____
_____
_____
_____
_____

KNOW...

Learning Objectives

1. Competitive advantage is a set of unique features of a company and its products that are perceived by the target market as significant and superior to the competition. They are cost, differentiation, and focus strategies. Cost competitive advantage is when a company is able to utilize its skilled workforce, inexpensive raw materials, controlled costs, and efficient operations to create maximum value to consumers. If a company's product or service has a valuable, unique offering for its consumers, then differentiation can occur. The third way a company can create a competitive advantage is through creating a focus. A focus competitive advantage seeks to understand and service the target market better than anyone else. Marketers use either cost leadership or differentiation to do that and often choose a niche or specific target market segment.

2. One of the very first steps in creating a marketing plan is the formation of a business mission statement. A mission statement should be worded according to a company's market, and not just about a specific product or service. A good mission statement should motivate all parties involved with the brand and create an opportunity for them to better understand the nature of the business, their advantage, and reason to exist. They also allow the marketer with a foundation that helps to shape the tone and character of the brand and marketing campaigns that will follow.

3. Once a business mission statement has been created, then it's important to conduct a situational analysis on the overall business environment to compete effectively. Businesses also have to research and analyze choices before choosing a path. Their decision-making process is called conducting a SWOT analysis, or situational analysis. SWOT stands for strengths, weaknesses, opportunities, and threats. A marketer must look at each part of the SWOT analysis to decide on the correct path and plans in order to create an effective marketing strategy.

4. After conducting a SWOT analysis and finding the strengths, weaknesses, opportunities, and threats for a product or brand, a company decides which strategic alternative will serve them the best. They can decide to penetrate the market of existing customers, find new markets to explore, develop new products, or push new products into new markets.

Key Terms

Competitive Advantage: The advantage over competitors gained by offering greater customer value, either through lower prices or by providing more benefits that justify higher prices.

Cost Leadership: Providing customers reasonable value at a lower price.

Differentiation: Delivering better benefits to your customer than anyone else. Companies typically achieve differentiation with *innovation, quality, or customer service.*

Diversification Strategy: A strategic alternative with the most risk where companies attempt to push into new markets and categories that may be beyond the company's comfort zone.

Environmental Scanning: Assesses the economic, cultural, demographic, political, ecological, and technological conditions and changes that exist in the environment.

Focus: Understanding and servicing your target market better than anyone else.

Market Development Strategy: A strategic alternative that concentrates on identifying and developing new markets and customers for their existing products and services.

Market Penetration Strategy: A strategic alternative that plans to increase profits by increasing market share among existing customers.

Marketing Myopia: This is the mistake of paying more attention to specific products of a company than the benefits and experiences produced by these products.

Mission Statement: A statement of the organization's purpose—what it wants to accomplish in the larger environment.

Product Development Strategy: A strategic alternative where companies create modified or new products to their existing markets.

Strategic Alternatives: The game plan that a company will choose in order to grow their share of market and get the largest growth and profits with the lowest risk. It is a portfolio planning tool for identifying growth opportunities in four different ways: market penetration, market development, product development, and diversification.

Sustainability: How long you are able to maintain your edge.

SWOT or Situational Analysis: A decision-making process used by marketers to assess the strengths, weaknesses, opportunities, and threats of their business environment.

Unique Selling Proposition or USP: Something that an organization is very good at but the competition is not.

Answers to Practice

Competitive Advantage: What Is it?
1. c   2. c   3. a   4. b   5. b

How to Develop a Business Mission Statement
1. b   2. b   3. d   4. a   5. c

What Is SWOT: Situation Analysis in Marketing
1. b   2. b   3. c   4. b   5. b

Types of Strategic Alternatives for Growth Opportunities
1. c   2. c   3. c   4. b   5. d

References

Armstrong, Gary; Kotler, Philip, Marketing: An Introduction, 13th Ed., ©2017. Reprinted and Electronically reproduced by permission of Pearson Education, Inc., New York, NY.

Armstrong, Kotler, Trifts, Buchwitz. (2017). *Marketing, An Introduction*. Pearson.

Barone, M.J. and T.E. DeCarlo (2003). "Emerging Forms of Competitive Advantage: Implications for Agricultural Producers." Midwest Agribusiness Trade Research and Information Center Research Paper 03-MRP 5.

Bruce, P. (October 11, 2016). Canada's best brands 2017: The top 25. *Canadian Business Magazine*. Retrieved from http://www.canadianbusiness.com/lists-and-rankings/best-brands/canadas-best-brands-2017-the-top-25/.

HBC.com. Retrieved from http://www3.hbc.com/hbc/about-us/.

Kimberley, A. (May 11, 2017). What Is competitive advantage? 3 Strategies that work. *The Balance*. Retrieved from https://www.thebalance.com/what-is-competitive-advantage-3-strategies-that-work-3305828.

Pellegrini, C. (October 30, 2015). Big Three telecom companies say they're winning the customer service battle. But are they? Financial Post. Retrieved from http://business.financialpost.com/technology/big-three-telecom-companies-say-theyre-winning-the-customer-service-battle-but-are-they/wcm/745d36f5-ca09-40e7-8650-005f7fe01e87.

Porter, M. (1998). *Competitive advantage, creating a sustaining, superior performance, Chapter 1*. Simon and Schuster. Retrieved from https://www.cirquedusoleil.com/en/about/global-citizenship/introduction/mission.aspx.

Thottam, I. (n.d.). 10 companies with awesome training and development programs, Monster.com, Retrieved from https://www.monster.com/career-advice/article/companies-with-awesome-training-development-programs.

9 Marketing Strategy

LEARNING OBJECTIVES

L01 Understand what strategic planning is and why it is important for the marketer to understand corporate strategy before commencing with the marketing strategy

L02 Know the steps involved in strategic planning

L03 Define marketing strategy

L04 Understand the marketing strategy process

L05 Know the internal influences that impact a marketer's strategy

L06 Know the external influences that impact a marketer's strategy

LEARN...

Every successful business must have a plan of attack or strategy.

This plan spells out the ways the company intends to rationalize its resources, engage in production, and even handle its clients. A sound business plan must also include a strategic marketing plan.

It takes a lot of time and effort to develop and maintain a marketing campaign that not only resonates with the intended target audience but creates a return on investment for the organization.

Strategic marketers strive to come up with and implement practical marketing campaigns that can guarantee a stable flow of business for the organization. Yet the development of a marketing campaign is more than "just creating pictures and words" that resonate with consumers. Like the company, marketing too, must create a plan of attack.

In order to do this, the marketing team must first be aligned and in tune with the overall objectives and strategies of the organization and be able to reinforce the company's mission in their communication campaigns. They need to be aware of who their "best fit" customer is and lastly, on constant alert of the internal and external influences that will impact a campaign and the company's bottom line.

Strategic Planning

 L01 Understand what strategic Planning is and why it is important for the marketer to understand corporate strategy before commencing with the marketing strategy

L02 Know the steps involved in strategic planning

Before commencing with the marketing strategy and plan, it is very important to be familiar with the "grand plan" of the company. Understanding the company's plan will define marketing's role and purpose.

Each company must define a game plan for long-run survival and growth that makes the most sense given its specific situation, opportunities, objectives, and resources. This is the focus of **strategic planning** and it is important to understand the company's plan's objectives before any of its business units (including marketing) begin their planning process

Armstrong et al. (2017) defines strategic planning as:

> *The process of developing and maintaining a strategic fit between the organization's goals and capabilities and its changing marketing opportunities.*

Company-wide strategic planning sets the stage and guides the rest of the planning within the firm. Companies usually prepare annual plans, long range plans, and strategic plans. The annual and long-range plans deal with the company's current business and how to keep them afloat and going. It's important that the whole of the organization is knowledgeable and cognizant of the corporate plan.

In contrast, the *strategic plans are more customer oriented* and involves adapting the firm to take advantage of opportunities that pop up in its constantly changing environment. Once the strategic plans are approved, it is important that the whole of the organization is familiar with the plans of the various business units.

At the corporate level, the company will start the strategic planning process by defining its overall purpose or mission. The mission details the strategic objectives and competitive scope that will guide the organization and should be market oriented and satisfy the needs of the customer. The company's senior management team will then decide what business units (or portfolios) and products are best for the company and how much support to give each one.

In turn, each business unit develops product(s) detailed marketing and other departmental plans that will support the company-wide plan (Figure 1).

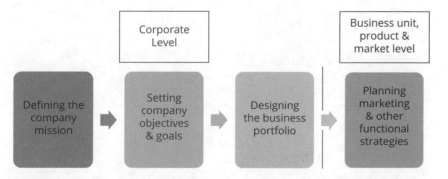

FIGURE 1 Steps in strategic planning. Marketing planning occurs at the business unit, product and market levels. It supports company strategic planning with more detailed plans for specific marketing opportunities.

Source: Based on Armstrong, Kotler, Trifts, Buchwitz, Marketing An Introduction, Pearson Canada, 2017.

Practice...

1. The strategy that the marketing develops is ultimately shaped by:
   a. the products and services developed by the competition.
   b. the goals and objectives of the company.
   c. the wishes of consumers.
   d. the customers who are deemed as a "best fit" by the company.

2. Strategic planning first starts at the:
   a. Corporate level
   b. Marketing level
   c. Business Unit level
   d. Customer level

3. Annual plans are more focused on:
   a. company's current business.
   b. the customer.
   c. the needs of the business unit.
   d. the needs of the market.

4. Strategic plans are more focussed on:
   a. the company.
   b. the customer.
   c. the company's mission.
   d. the "grand plan" of the company.

5. At the Business Unit level, the marketer is responsible for:
   a. designing the business portfolio.
   b. defining the company mission.
   c. setting company objectives and goals.
   d. planning marketing and other functional strategies.

 # Apply...

1. In groups, write a mission statement for your new company—a cleaning service for urban condo dwellers. Name your company and present your mission statement to the class. To get an idea of the steps of drafting a mission statement, click on the following link: https://tinyurl.com/flextext-mission

   _____

   _____

   _____

   _____

   _____

   _____

   _____

   _____

   _____

   _____

   _____

   _____

   _____

2. In groups, set two corporate objectives and two marketing objectives for your cleaning company. Present your objectives to the class. Not sure what to include as corporate or objectives. Click on the following link to learn what they are: https://tinyurl.com/flextext-corp-objectives. To learn more about marketing objectives, click on the following link: https://tinyurl.com/flextext-marketing

   _____

   _____

   _____

   _____

   _____

   _____

   _____

   _____

   _____

   _____

   _____

   _____

   _____

What Is Marketing Strategy?

 Define marketing strategy

L04 Understand the marketing strategy process

The strategic plan (as mentioned) outlines the company's overall mission and objectives. Marketing's role and activities aim to reinforce the company's goals by managing a customer-driven strategy, as shown in the Figure 2.

At the center of every organization's business exist customers and the goal for every business is to create value for their customers and build profitable relationships with them. Once we have a customer, we can then start to devise a **marketing strategy**:

> *the marketing logic by which the company hopes to create this customer value and achieve these profitable relationships.*
> (Armstrong et al., 2017)

The marketing strategy is shaped by the ultimate goals of the company and it is these goals that serve as the foundation of the marketing plan. The marketing plan is a blueprint developed by the marketing team of an organization that describes how their **products** and/or **services** will be offered to customers.

Products are:

> *tangible items that are offered to a market for attention, acquisition, use or consumption that might satisfy a want or a need produced by labour to satisfy a need.* (Armstrong, 2018, p. 680)

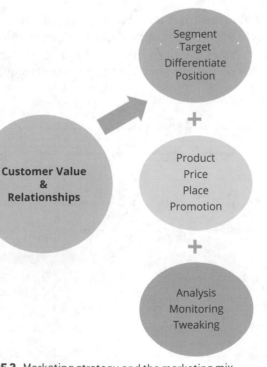

FIGURE 2 Marketing strategy and the marketing mix diagram.

Source: Based on Armstrong et al, Marketing Strategy & the Marketing Mix Diagram, Marketing An Introduction, Pearson Canada, 2017, Pearson Canada, 2017, 58.

A service is:

an activity, benefit or satisfaction offered for sale that is essentially intangible and does not result in the ownership of anything. (Armstrong et al., 2017)

The marketing team looks at the market as a whole and decides which customers will serve them best and be a "best fit" for their products and services. This is done by segmenting and targeting of the core customer. These smaller segments are then differentiated based on their geography, demography, psychography, and/or behaviour type. The aim of the marketer at this stage is to satisfy the "best fit" customers and positioning the product and service to them.

Now that the ideal customer segments are identified, the company will design an integrated marketing communication mix that targets the "best fit" consumer made up of factors under its control—product, place, price, and promotion—also known as the four Ps. To find the best marketing strategy and mix, the company engages in marketing analysis, planning, implementation, and control.

Once the plan is designed, it is implemented and constantly analyzed. This analysis presents an opportunity for the marketing team to gauge the reaction of competitors, suppliers, intermediaries, and consumers to the campaign and to see if their plan is working and if tweaks are necessary. *"Through these activities, the company watches and adapts to the actors and forces in the marketing environment . . ."* (Armstrong et al., 2017) that will affect their relationship with the customer.

While marketing strategies vary from company to company the process described above is fairly consistent for most companies and it allows them the chance to connect and understand their customers and to grow their market share and revenue.

Last but not least, marketing strategies to reach customers are influenced by internal and external forces which will be discussed in the next section.

Practice...

1. At the center of every organization's business there exists:
   a. a positioning.
   b. a customer value and relationship.
   c. a differentiating factor.
   d. a corporate mission.

2. In most cases, products are:
   a. intangible.
   b. tangible.
   c. controlled by suppliers and distributors.
   d. developed as a direct response to competitive forces.

3. In most cases, services are:
   a. intangible.
   b. tangible.
   c. controlled by suppliers and distributors.
   d. developed as a direct response to competitive forces.

4. The main goal for every business should be:
   a. to make a profit.
   b. a return on their investment.
   c. a happy workforce and environment.
   d. to create value for their customers and build profitable relationships with them.

5. The strategy that the marketing develops is ultimately shaped by:
   a. the products and services developed by the competition.
   b. the goals and objectives of the company.
   c. the wishes of consumers.
   d. the customers who are deemed as a "best fit" by the company.

Apply...

1. In groups, present your findings to the class.

   Develop a strategy and marketing mix for your own restaurant. The market is cluttered, so it's important that you distinguish and differentiate yourself. Refer to Marketing Strategy and Marketing Mix matrix. Not sure what is trending? Click on the following link to learn about some popular foods now in the marketplace: https://tinyurl.com/flextext-food-trends

   - What are the main aspects of your restaurant that you will market in order to make it successful? (Why should people come to your restaurant?)
   - Who is the ideal customer for your restaurant?
   - What's a suitable name for your restaurant?

to be continued

Apply...

continued

2. In groups, present your findings to the class.

What's your restaurant's marketing mix? Make sure to address each of the four P's.

_____

_____

_____

_____

_____

_____

_____

_____

_____

_____

_____

_____

_____

_____

_____

_____

_____

_____

_____

_____

_____

_____

_____

_____

_____

_____

_____

_____

_____

_____

Internal Influences on Marketing Strategy

L05 Know the internal influences that impact a marketer's strategy

Marketing plans are not finite. Every marketing department and organization is affected by a variety of influences either from within the company or from the outside.

Marketing is very vulnerable and effected by internal influences. From the ideals of the managers, to the simple practicality of the product's use, much of what guides the marketing department comes from the company itself. A marketing campaign is only as good as the company behind it, and as a marketer, you have to constantly ensure that the marketing plan ties back to, and matches, the goals, will, and abilities of the organization. In many ways, these **internal influences**, also known as the **internal environment**, can often shape the marketing plan.

The following are some of the influences that shape the marketing strategy.

Quality of Good and Support

Can my product continue to stand up to the needs of my customer?

Many marketers will look within their organization to see if the product or service that they are marketing is of quality and if it consistently delivers value to its customers.

The marketer's goal is to help customers feel confident about the choice they've made or about to make. Providing an advertisement or a mobile message often just doesn't help. Instead, marketers need to make sure that they understand their customer, provide them with the right product, and support and continuously develop and enhance their offer.

Intuit, for example, has made a concerted effort to provide a quality product to its target customers with its TurboTax software product. When it comes to preparing taxes, consumers have a bewildering range of choices, from accountants to software programs, to doing it with pencil and paper. Intuit has made a concerted effort to help "do it yourself" consumers by providing them with easy online communities that match the customer's profile, a 24/7 customer service email and telephone number, unfiltered user reviews, and a "help me choose" function that allows consumers to go through a 30-second "check the boxes that apply" exercise and guides them to the product that suits them most as well as a justification to *why* that product is the best choice (Spenner, 2012).

In short, the TurboTax software is valuable to consumers who prepare their tax returns themselves because they present a quality product which matters greatly to its consumers.

Human Resources and Culture

You've got an amazing marketing campaign planned. There's just one problem. You can't pull it off.

If you are the extent of the marketing department or worse, if your marketing department is rather inept, then you stand no chance of being able to succeed with your objectives.

Your marketing team's and the company's ability to actually perform the work is a very important internal influence on any marketing campaign.

Human resources and the culture of the company can affect marketing internally. A motivated and well-trained workforce can deliver market-leading customer service and productivity to create a competitive marketing advantage. A business with highly skilled employees and a collaborative firm culture tends to have a higher rate of successful implementation simply because employees are invested in its success and willing to share ideas to achieve its stated goals. Companies that are well known for their recruiting and culture include Google, WestJet, and the Great Little Box Company.

Budget

You have the most impressive marketing campaign for your product or service but if your total marketing budget is only 1,000 dollars, how do you proceed?

If this is the case, then your campaign strategy might only remain an idea.

Part of the budgeting process includes deciding how much money to allocate to different media, as well as the frequency (or number of times) in which you advertise or promote your product.

If the budget allocated by the company to marketing is limited, then placing an ad in a community newsletter might make more sense than creating a television commercial or placing an ad in any expensive magazine like Maclean's or Time. A limited budget can also affect the frequency (or number of times) in which you advertise and promote your product or service.

Corporate Objectives

You have a brilliant marketing idea, unfortunately the company president thinks it's a little too risqué.

Chick-fil-A, a well-known fast food restaurant in the United States that specializes in chicken sandwiches is not open on Sunday due to the religious beliefs of the company's founders. Despite the fact that plenty of marketing research, as well as social media campaigns, show that there is no business reason to stay closed on Sundays, this chain still does.

Why? At its core, it is a corporate belief of the firm to stay true to the founder's beliefs. These corporate objectives are set by the leadership of an organization and supersede all other objectives.

Not all corporate objectives are established on the morality of the founders but as a rule, marketing must follow the lead of corporate objectives, or the goals set by the corporate officers of the organization. Some corporate objectives may include not advertising in certain forms of media or not marketing to certain demographic groups.

Source: James R. Martin/Shutterstock.

In any event, marketing objectives cannot overrule corporate ones.

Practice...

1. What is an example of a corporate objective?
   a. Having a small marketing budget
   b. Targeting the right market
   c. Ability to execute a marketing plan
   d. Staying closed on a Sunday

2. Which is the best definition of internal influences on marketing?
   a. Guidance from corporate
   b. Guiding influences for the marketing department from the company itself
   c. Practicality of use
   d. Limits based on marketing

3. Which of these is NOT an internal influence on marketing?
   a. Corporate objectives
   b. Marketing budget
   c. Language use of target audience
   d. Abilities of the marketing department

4. Which of these is an example of a team being unable to execute a marketing plan because of internal influences?
   a. Conflicting with the law
   b. Not having enough people to do the work necessary
   c. Conflicting with a corporate objective
   d. Targeting rich people instead of middle class people

5. Which of these is an example of the quality of good influencing marketing?
   a. Marketing that is matched to corporate objectives
   b. A luxury services firm choosing whom to target
   c. Marketing that is matched to budget
   d. Marketing that is matched to a manager's objectives

 # Apply...

1. In small groups, address the following question then be prepared to present to the class.

   In your opinion, why is it important for the firm's marketing strategy (plan) to be based upon the firm's internal environment?

   _____

   _____

   _____

   _____

   _____

   _____

   _____

   _____

   _____

   _____

   _____

   _____

   _____

   _____

   _____

2. In small groups, address the following question then be prepared to present to the class. Tim Horton's (http://www.timhortons.com/ca/en/index.php) is considering to starting selling and delivering pizza. Does this sound like a good idea for them based on their current marketing strategy? Explain.

   _____

   _____

   _____

   _____

   _____

   _____

   _____

   _____

   _____

   _____

   _____

   _____

   _____

External Influences on Marketing Strategy

L06   Know the external influences that impact a marketer's strategy

All businesses are exposed to the outside world, and, given the number and variety of external variables in existence today, the decision-making of a company is frequently influenced. Any force outside of the company's employees, leadership, and business strategy that can affect an organization's performance can be considered an **external influence**. External influences are sometimes so powerful—for example, if the economy slips into a depression and consumer spending plummets—that the original marketing strategy becomes untenable and must be completely revised.

There are six external factors known as PESTLE that influence the marketing strategy of a business or organization:

1.   Political

2.   Economic

3.   Social

4.   Technological

5.   Legal

6.   Environmental

Another external factor that can influence a business is competition making the external factors, seven in total.

Some organizations may perform PESTLE to obtain information on major external influences on their business.

PESTLE analysis greatly influences the marketing environment of a product or service and helps to determine the strategies that will be adopted by the marketing team. It works alongside the situational (SWOT) analysis in determining the external factors (that is, the threats and opportunities) that may influence strategy or marketing campaign.

Political Influences

Political influences can affect how consumers purchase their products.

If a company seems to support one specific political party over another, the company may alienate potential customers. For instance, if a company publicly supports a Liberal, Conservative, or NDP official, they may unknowingly persuade their customers into or out of buying their products. In the 2015 Canadian federal election, for example, the Torstar newspapers publicly endorsed the Liberal party, while the Post media newspapers endorsed the Conservative party (National Post, 2015; Thestar.com, 2015).

An endorsement such as this could affect circulation rates, as well as advertising revenue for the newspaper.

Source: Arindambanerjee /Shutterstock.

Economic Influences

The economy influences marketing strategy in a number of ways. The state of the economy and our environment has a major influence on consumer buying power. If the economy is experiencing a recession, consumers may not be able to buy what they normally buy due to lack of employment. If a person is laid off and is in danger of depleting their savings, they may rethink buying the large cup of coffee they purchase at Starbucks on the way to work every day. Instead, they may start making their coffee at home. This change will eventually affect Starbucks' bottom line.

Some marketers like Gold's Gym took advantage of the economic recession in the United States by running an ad that said "'You can't control the economy but you can control how many push-ups you do and take control where you can, and we can help you." That's a powerful message (Forbes, 2008).

Social Influences

Demographic and lifestyle information of an area should be gathered frequently to ensure the success of any marketing campaign. Today marketers are aware that their consumer groups live online. Given the velocity with which a message can be disseminated and amplified across the internet, coupled with the impact of mobile technologies, more economic buyers can be reached in a fraction of the time than it once took.

Staying on top of characteristics such as age, income, race, religion, population size, and education are key factors in a business understanding who to serve and how to serve them. Also, marketers need to track those who influence social behaviour and partner with social influencers who are aligned with their ideals.

Technological Influences

Technology is always changing and this frequent change has a significant effect on how a business operates. Many consumers take advantage of the convenience of shopping daily. The ability to purchase products online has changed consumer spending. According to CIRA, "Canadians have embraced electronic commerce and plan to continue to spend $39 billion online by 2019, representing 9.5% of all retail purchases in Canada. Statistics Canada's data (in their most recent data on the topic) reports that Canadian companies sold more than $136 billion in goods and services online in 2013, up from $122 billion a year earlier" (CIRA, 2016).

As a result, several companies advertise incentives such as free shipping inside their stores and on store websites because they have recognized the increase in online shopping.

Legal Influences

Federal and state regulations on a specific industry can also influence how a company performs. For instance, in the alcoholic beverage industry, would it be sensible to have children under the age of 18 in advertisements selling alcoholic beverages if it is against the law for minors to consume alcohol?

Environmental Influences

An increased focus on environmental issues has contributed to a rise in the demand for environment-friendly products and services. Also known as *"green marketing"*, companies today seek to go above and beyond traditional marketing by promoting environmental core values in the hope that consumers will associate these values with their company or brand. Engaging in these sustainable activities can lead to creating a new product line that caters to a new target market.

There are a large number of environmental questions impacting marketing, services, and the production of products, for example:

- Does your production, sourcing of materials, packaging, and distribution impact the environment?
- Can minimum levels of packaging and environment friendly packaging be achieved without compromising product quality or appeal?
- Are your suppliers as environmentally friendly as your organization?
- Are your consumers willing to pay more for environmentally friendly products?

It is rare these days to see an organisation that has not adapted their marketing strategies to capitalise on the consumer appetite for environment-friendly products and services. Companies like Ben and Jerry's, Whole Foods, and Starbucks are just some of the companies that have employed green marketing strategies, stressing the sustainability of their products or the green methods employed in their packaging or retail stores.

Source: Atstock Productions/Shutterstock.

Competitive Influences

In any industry, a business should consider who their competitors are. This research should be factored into the marketing plan and strategy because the information gathered on your competitors' products, supply chains, pricing, and marketing tactics can determine what sets you apart from the pack, what products and/or services to offer your consumers, and how to offer them.

Some companies make bad business decisions because they fail to research their competition. One of the reasons the United States, mega-retailer Target failed in Canada, was because of its failure to assess the Canadian landscape and the retailers who were vying for a piece of the consumer's wallet. In reverse, when Target announced its arrival to Canada, it allowed retail competitors like Walmart, Shoppers Drug Mart, Canadian Tire, and Joe Fresh, the opportunity to assess their Target competitor and improve and better their store operations and offers to customers (Kolm, 2015).

Practice…

1. Identify the seven external influences on a company's marketing strategy.
   a. Social, Technology, Politics, Economy, Competition, Environment, and Legal
   b. Consumers, Leadership, Competition, Social, Legal, Ecology, and Technology
   c. Leadership, Politics, Consumers, Legal, Technology, Corporate, and Taxes
   d. Competition, Employees, Leadership, Consumers, Political, Social, and Technology

2. A business that sells toys should open a store in a location that has a large population of _____.
   a. college students
   b. single professionals
   c. seniors
   d. young families

3. A plan developed by an organization that consists of the company's product/service mix and how that product/service will be offered to consumers is referred to as a _____.
   a. marketing strategy
   b. promotional mix
   c. marketing mix
   d. company goal

4. Analyze the situation that should NOT be considered an external influence on a company's marketing strategy.
   a. My company just hired five IT professionals.
   b. Over the last 5 years, 12 colleges have opened in South Florida.
   c. The population of Sampletown, BC, has decreased by 20%.
   d. The new Samsung cell phone will be in stores next week.

5. Which of the following should a pizza company least consider when finding a location for their business?
   a. Average household income
   b. Average household age
   c. Total number of residents
   d. Average number of pets per home

Apply...

1. In groups, answer this question and present your answer to the class.

   As the marketing manager for XYZ Tobacco, a new tobacco company, you have been asked to assess the external environmental influences that will impact your new electronic cigarette (vaporizer) business. Perform a PESTLE analysis for your business, as well as a listing of all the competitors in your market. Here are some facts about "vaping": https://tinyurl.com/flextext-vaping

to be continued

 # Apply...

continued

2. In groups, produce a list of all your immediate competitors in the vapor market and indicate why you believe they may hinder your success.

_____

_____

_____

_____

_____

_____

_____

_____

_____

_____

_____

_____

_____

_____

_____

_____

_____

_____

KNOW...

Learning Objectives

1. Armstrong defines strategic planning as "*The process of developing and maintaining a strategic fit between the organization's goals and capabilities and its changing marketing opportunities.*"

    Before a marketing plan is developed, a company must first define its mission, set company objectives and goals, design the business portfolio, and then pass the baton over to the business units to come up with strategies to support their line of business.

2. Marketing strategy is shaped by the ultimate goals of the company and it is these goals that serve as the foundation of the marketing plan. The marketing plan is a blueprint developed by the marketing team of an organization that describes how their products and/or services will be offered to customers. At the core of every strategy are customers, which companies aim to build relationships with and value for. Within the group of customers are customers who are "best fits" for the various products and services. These smaller segments are then differentiated and the aim of the marketer at this stage is to satisfy the "best fit" customers and to position the company's products and services to them. Once the ideal customer segments are identified, the company will design an integrated marketing mix made up of factors under its control—product, place, price, and promotion—also known as the four Ps.

3. It is often those internal influences, coming from within the company itself, that really make or break a marketing strategy. First a company should know their target market and be able to market them with a quality product at a suitable price. They also need to be able to properly execute a marketing plan and have the right team and financial capabilities. Finally, they need to make sure that any marketing plans do not go against any existing corporate objectives.

4. Businesses must have the ability to adapt to any external influence that can alter the company's ultimate goals. Staying current on competitive, political, social, legal, economic, technological, and environmental (PESTLE) external influences will help a business in developing a successful marketing strategy that will increase the likeliness of longevity.

Key Terms

External Influences: Any force outside of the company's employees, leadership, and business strategy that can affect an organization's performance can be considered an external influence. These forces include politics, economy, technology, environment, social, legal, and competition.

Internal Influences: Influences from within the company that affect the strategy and planning process. These influences include corporate objectives, budget, human resources, culture, and quality of good and support services.

Marketing Strategy: The reasoning and plan of attack that marketers use in order to create customer value and profitable relationships with customers.

Products: Anything tangible that can be offered to a market that might satisfy a want or need.

Service: Anything intangible, such as an activity or benefit, that might satisfy a want or need and that can be offered for sale to a market without it resulting in ownership.

Strategic Planning: *"The process of developing and maintaining a strategic fit between the organization's goals and capabilities and its changing marketing opportunities."*

Answers to Practice

Strategic Planning

Understand what strategic planning is and why it is important for the marketer to understand corporate strategy before commencing with the marketing strategy.

Know the steps involved in strategic planning

1. b   2. a   3. a   4. b   5. d

What Is Marketing Strategy?

Define marketing strategy

Understand the marketing strategy process

1. b   2. b   3. a   4. d   5. b

Internal Influences on Marketing Strategy
1. d   2. b   3. c   4. a   5. b

External Influences on Marketing Strategy
1. a   2. d   3. a   4. a   5. d

References

Armstrong, Gary; Kotler, Philip, Marketing: An Introduction, 13th Ed., ©2017. Reprinted and Electronically reproduced by permission of Pearson Education, Inc., New York, NY.

Armstrong et al. (2018). *Marketing: An Introduction* (Updated 6th Canadian Edition with Integrated B2B Case). Don Mills, Ontario: Pearson Canada.

CIRA, The State of e-Commerce in Canada, CIRA Internet Factbook, p. 2, March 2016.

Knowledge Wharton, Forbes. (December 1, 2008). Retrieved from https://www.forbes.com/2008/12/01/advertising-recession-wharton-ent-salescx_1201whartonadvertising.html.

Kolm, J. (January 16, 2015). Did target understand the Canadian market? Strategy. Retrieved from http://strategyonline.ca/2015/01/16/did-target-understand-the-canadian-market/.

National Post View: Our choice for government. *National Post*. Retrieved October 17, 2015.

Spenner, P., Freeman, K. (May 2012). To keep your customers, keep it simple. *Harvard Business Review*.

Toronto Star endorses Liberal Leader Justin Trudeau for prime minister. (October 9, 2015). *Thestar.com*. Retrieved October 14, 2015.

Integrated Marketing Communication (IMC) and the Marketing Plan

LEARNING OBJECTIVES

LO1 Identify the Integrated marketing mix and its tools

LO2 Define integrated marketing communications and its importance in marketing strategy

LO3 Differentiate between push and pull strategies

LO4 Identify the nature and purpose of each promotion tool

LEARN...

In order to compete in today's difficult market, a marketing manager must create not just a promotional mix, but an integrated marketing communications plan. This is a coordinating plan of promotional messages for a product to ensure consistency. The product's promotional message should be consistent and create an overall integrated theme. By integrating tools such as advertising, direct mail, social media, telemarketing, and sales promotion, you provide clarity, consistency, and maximum communications impact.

In the traditional approach to marketing communications, businesses and their agencies plan separate campaigns for advertising, press relations, direct marketing, and sales promotions. Integrated campaigns use the same communication tools to reinforce each other and improve marketing effectiveness. In an integrated campaign, you can use advertising to raise awareness of a product and generate leads for the sales force. By communicating the same information in press releases and feature articles, you reinforce the messages in the advertising. You can then use direct mail or email to follow-up inquiries from the advertising or press campaigns and provide prospects with more information. To help convert those prospects to customers, you can use telemarketing to sell directly or make appointments for the sales team.

Integrated Marketing Mix

LO1 Identify the Integrated marketing mix and its tools

After deciding on a marketing strategy, the company is ready to begin its positioning in the marketplace with a mix of tactical tools known as the marketing mix. According to Armstrong et al., the **marketing mix** is . . .

The set of controllable, tactical marketing tools that the firm blends to produce the response it wants in the target market. (Armstrong et al., 2017)

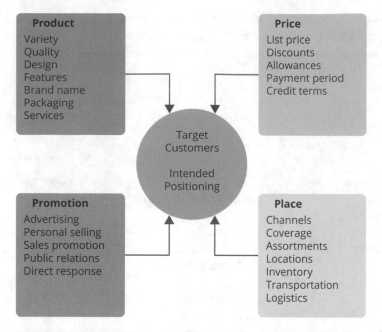

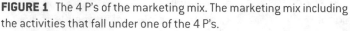

FIGURE 1 The 4 P's of the marketing mix. The marketing mix including the activities that fall under one of the 4 P's.

Source: Armstrong, Gary, Kotler, Philip, Marketing: An Introduction, 13th Ed., ©2017. Reprinted and Electronically reproduced by permission of Pearson Education, Inc., New York, NY.

The marketing mix consists of all the activities or tools, that a firm can resort to in order to influence the demand for its product. These tools (demonstrated in the Figure 1) can be grouped into four categories known as the **4 P's— product, price, place, and promotion**.

- **Product:** It refers to what the company is offering the market. The product can be a tangible or intangible good, service, or a combination of both. For example, well known Canadian clothing retailer Roots is well known for their various clothing apparel, including leather jackets. In this case, a Roots leather jacket which comes in a variety of styles and sizes to appease its customers would be the product.

- **Price:** It refers to the cost a customer must pay to obtain the product. The final price a consumer pays for a product includes all extra time and effort that was put into bringing the product to the consumer's hands. Roots will calculate a suggested retail price for its jacket that is based on the current economy and what the competition has set as a price for a similar product. Depending on the popularity and complexity of the jacket (that is, patches, colours, type of leather), the price may also be affected.

- **Place:** The distribution of the product and the availability of the service. Roots has over 200 retail locations around the world, a strong online presence, and 40 outlet stores across Canada, where consumers can purchase leather jackets and other Roots products (https://roots.com/on/demandware.store).

- **Promotion:** The activities that communicate the merits of the product or service and persuade consumers to purchase it. Roots runs advertisements in a variety of magazines and newspapers, as well as on television. It has in store merchandising a strong social media presence that encourages consumers to engage with the brand and has been an official sponsor and clothier of the Canadian and American Olympic teams.

An effective marketing plan blends all the components (the 4 P's) of the marketing mix into an integrated marketing communication program that aims to achieve the company's objectives by delivering value to its customers.

Practice...

1. The marketing mix consists of:
   a. planning, profit, product, and price.
   b. product, personnel, profit, and price.
   c. product, place, promotion, and price.
   d. product, profit, place, and promotion.

2. The five types of promotion are:
   a. advertising, public relations, direct response, product, and promotion.
   b. advertising, public relations, direct response, sales promotion, and personal selling.
   c. purchase, product, place, price and profit, and persuasion.
   d. advertising, promotion, sales, pricing, and profit.

3. The price of a product includes _____
   a. amount charged to the purchaser.
   b. the financial amount charged plus the time and effort put forth by the purchaser.
   c. the amount of product sold to each customer.
   d. only what the retailer paid for it.

4. The sponsorship of the Canadian Olympic team would fall under:
   a. promotions.
   b. place.
   c. product.
   d. advertising.

5. Products are:
   a. tangible.
   b. intangible.
   c. both tangible and intangible.
   d. the most important features of a brand.

 **Apply...**

1. Individually, list several shopping products that you recently acquired. Can't remember what a shopping product is? Click here for a definition: https://tinyurl.com/flextext-shopping. Which element of the 4 P's was most influential in your purchasing decision? Present to the class.

_____

_____

_____

_____

_____

_____

_____

_____

_____

_____

_____

2. In teams of four, use each of the 4 P's to discuss how Tim Horton's implements its marketing strategy. How have they modified place and products over the past 5 years? Present to class.

_____

_____

_____

_____

_____

_____

_____

_____

_____

_____

_____

_____

_____

Integrated Marketing Communications (IMC)

LO2 Define integrated marketing communications and its importance in marketing strategy

As mentioned previously, consumers today are showered with commercial messages from a variety of sources. They are not privy to the marketer's communication objectives nor are they familiar with their strategy and message intent. They just store the information under the company brand and tend not to differentiate by product(s), service(s), source, or promotional approach.

If the messages from these sources conflict or differ, it can lead to customer confusion and possibly attrition. It's akin to receive mixed messages from someone who one day acts like they're your best friend and the next day, ignores you. In marketing, it's analogous to a campaign where on the same day a company will launch a television ad which focuses on their product's attribute, place a local newspaper ad to push the product's lowest price in the market or share an Instagram post about an upcoming event or recent sponsorship.

This confusion and lack of consistency may be due to a lack of communication from within the organization or between external partners like advertising agencies or public relations (PR) firms but the reality is that customers do not care nor do they differentiate brands by internal departments, external partners, or communication tools. They see the brand as a whole and any inconsistency in communication could create a blurred brand perception and possibly an end to the relationship.

Most companies have realized how important it is to have a cohesive marketing communication plan and prefer to adopt an **IMC** or **integrated marketing communications** plan. The concept is commonly practiced

Carefully Blended Mix of Promotion Tools

FIGURE 2 Integrated marketing communications. A company must carefully integrate its many communications to deliver a clear, consistent, and compelling message about a company and its brands.

Source: Taken from Armstrong, Kotler, Trifts, Buchwitz. *Marketing, An Introduction*, Pearson Canada, 2017.

throughout most organizations, marketing departments, and agencies, with the belief that all promotional messages to consumers should be integrated. This means that:

> the company must carefully integrate its many communication channels to deliver a clear, consistent and compelling message about the organization and its brands. (Armstrong et al., 2017)

At the end of the day, an IMC messaging strategy reaching any of the **five touch points of the promotional part of the marketing mix** (advertising, public relations, personal selling, sales promotion, and direct response) should *focus on being consistent from a creative and key theme perspective, regardless of it being a television ad, magazine article, coupon, or social media site.*

Practice...

1. Why are integrated marketing communication plans so important to marketers?
   a. There are many options now for promotional messages using online social media and alternative advertising methods.
   b. They ensure consistency at every customer contact point with the message.
   c. There are many promotional marketing options available to marketers today such as online social media and alternative advertising methods.
   d. They are the best option available to sales teams when pitching clients

2. IMC is an acronym for:
   a. Institutional Management Consultant
   b. International Marketing Consultant
   c. Integrated Marketing Communications
   d. Integrated Marketing Condition

3. How would a new condominium development company implement IMC in their sales promotions?
   a. By stressing to their sales staff that they have to close the deal by using traditional techniques
   b. By designing a billboard that will be located on a busy commuter route
   c. By ensuring that their street display ads all have the same image and theme as their TV, radio, and magazine advertising
   d. By asking viewers of the condominium suites to post "likes" on their Facebook and Instagram pages

4. The five touch points of the promotional marketing mix are:
   a. product, price, place, promotion, and purchase.
   b. product, price, purchase, promotion, and personal selling.
   c. advertising, public relations, personal selling, sales promotion, and direct response.
   d. marketing, advertising, public relations, personal selling, and sales promotion.

5. In the marketing mix, the five touch points fall under which part of the marketing mix.
   a. Product
   b. Promotions
   c. Price
   d. Place

Apply...

1. In groups of two, provide an example of an IMC campaign that caught your eye. Name all the IMC tools that were used by the marketer. Present your campaign example to class.

_____

_____

_____

_____

_____

_____

_____

_____

_____

_____

_____

_____

_____

_____

_____

2. Describe how an IMC campaign is integrated by providing an example. Not sure what one looks like? Click on the following link (https://tinyurl.com/flextext-integrated) to view how Porsche integrated an IMC campaign.

_____

_____

_____

_____

_____

_____

_____

_____

_____

_____

_____

_____

_____

_____

_____

Promotion Strategies

L03 Differentiate between push and pull strategies

So, your company is ready to bring its latest product to the market. There's just one little problem, no one knows you exist. Even though consumers have so much choice, it still is difficult for them to find and incorporate new products and services into their lifestyle and habits.

There are two different strategies—pull and push—that will help to put your product into the hands and minds of consumers.

Pull Strategy

Pull strategy is:

> *a promotion strategy that induces final consumers to buy the product, creating a demand vacuum that "pulls" the product through the channel.* (Armstrong et al., 2017)

Marketers use pull strategies to get the word out and induce customers to buy a product. They use the advertising, consumer promotions, and direct and digital tools to create value for their consumers and then draw or "pull" them to a product or service. Furthermore, the aim of a successful pull strategy is to force retailers to seek out and stock products that in essence customers can pull out of the retailer's hands.

For example, the Fidget spinner toy craze of 2017 was marketed on social media and YouTube channels to predominately younger Gen Y viewers. The spinner demonstrations and promotions on these channels created such a strong pull from this younger target market that it forced most major retailers to seek out the product and stock it in their stores.

Source: MNStudio/Shutterstock.

The fidget spinner toy craze pulled in the young Gen Y audience with a nontraditional digital promotion that included YouTube and many social media channels.

Push Promotion

Let's be realistic—you may obsess over fidget spinners but chances are that many of your potential clients lack your enthusiasm. In fact, there are probably a fair amount of potential customers who don't know the difference between one spinner and another and just blindly walk into stores saying that any old spinner will do. So, how do you engage them? In short, through push promotion.

A **push strategy** relies on the fact that the customer has already made the choice to purchase a product but now you the marketer, have to push your product (not the competitor's) into their hands. A push promotion strategy involves *"pushing a product through marketing channels to final consumers"* (Armstrong, Kotler, Trifts, et al., 2011, p. 476).Through the use of personal selling and trade promotion, the producer pushes the product to channel members, which in turn promote it to final customers. For example, few people walk into a mattress store like Sleep Country Canada knowing what they want. A sales person assists them with product information and encourages them to try several different models like Sealy or Serta and then find the one they like. In short, they are pushing different mattresses until a satisfactory one is found. However, push promotion doesn't just target the final consumer. Remember that companies like Sealy and Serta have to convince retailers like Sleep Country Canada to carry their goods and promote or "push" them to final customers. As a result, trade shows, free samples, and building good relationships with retailers are some of the ways that companies use for push promotion.

Overall, with pull promotion you might find that customers pulled in your marketing communication and then did a lot of the work of demanding that stores carry your goods. However, with push promotion, you as a marketer and producer of a product have got to focus in and convince retailers, that your products will sell to the final consumer.

Lesson Summary

In this lesson, we learned about the differences between push promotion and pull promotion. Remember that you can think of push promotion as pushing a product or service into the hands of consumers, while pull promotion is more like consumers pulling it from you. Pull promotion makes extensive use of reputation, and therefore, often is based on print or online advertising, or word of mouth. Push promotion, on the other hand, doesn't make such a big deal out of brand, and indeed is more focused on putting your goods into the hands of potential users. Trade shows, free samples, and in-store demos are examples of push promotion.

Practice...

1. Which of these tools would a company use to complement its pull advertising strategy?
   a. Online ads
   b. Free samples
   c. Trade shows
   d. Showrooms

2. Which of these is most true?
   a. Push promotion gets its name because consumers push for new goods.
   b. Pull promotion gets its name because companies pull consumers in with trade shows.
   c. Push promotion gets its name because companies push goods onto potential clients.
   d. None of the above.

3. Which of these products is most likely to use an integrated pull promotion in order to attract customers?
   a. Mobile phones
   b. Carpets
   c. Picture frames
   d. Door stops

4. Which of these tools would a company use to complement its push promotion strategy?
   a. Online ads
   b. Free samples
   c. Trade shows
   d. Show rooms

5. Which of these businesses would most likely use a push promotion strategy to engage a sales force?
   a. Mobile phones
   b. Gaming systems
   c. Restaurants
   d. Mattresses

 # Apply...

1. In groups of two, employ a push strategy to promote the upcoming iPhone 8. What elements would you use? Click on this link to view some of the potential new specs for this phone: https://tinyurl.com/flextext-iphone

_____

_____

_____

_____

_____

_____

_____

_____

_____

_____

_____

2. In groups of two, employ a pull strategy to promote the upcoming iPhone 8. What elements would you use?

_____

_____

_____

_____

_____

_____

_____

_____

_____

_____

_____

Promotion Tools

LO4 Identify the nature and purpose of each promotion tool

An integrated marketing communications plan is a coordination of all promotional tools for a product or service to ensure consistency at every customer contact point. After selecting a push or pull strategy, the marketer will decide on the tools that will shape their communication to consumers. They need to also recognize that with IMC, each of these tools is not a stand-alone discipline but rather, one of the pieces that will complement the consumer's decision-making process and ultimately drive sales.

Advertising

Advertising is a key component of promotion and is usually one of the most visible elements of an integrated marketing communications program. It is defined as:

> *a paid form of marketing communication through the media that is designed to influence the thought patterns and purchase behaviour of a target audience.* (Tuckwell, 2015, p. 6)

Most integrated marketing communications plans start out with a cohesive advertising plan. Marketers prefer advertising because of its ability to reach large audiences at a low cost, as well as its ability to create an emotion through its artful use of sound, colour, visuals, and print. Some of the drawbacks related to advertising are that it can be very costly, is impersonal, and hard to measure its success with regard to return on investment.

From an IMC perspective, the company's message when advertising should be prominently featured across all media and reinforce a consistent message. In 2016, Canada Goose launched its "Out There" campaign to persuade 25–45 year old "on the go" adults to buy their coats. The campaign was consistent across over 40 markets that it had selected. Using traditional television and radio spots, Canada Goose aired the same—one 2-minute film and two 15-second films—on out of home billboards and digital display ads in busy retail locations like Harrods, airports like Toronto's Billy Bishop, and London's Knightsbridge Station. The ad showed two actors wearing their parkas and walking the cold and rugged terrain of Newfoundland. The spots reinforced the parka's warmth and durability and the brand's "Made in Canada" positioning and commitment (Singh, 2016).

IMC Plan—Public Relations

Public relations or PR provides an organization or individual exposure to their audiences using topics of public interest and news items that usually do not require direct payment. Public relations is the practice of managing an organization's communication to strengthen relations between the organization and its different publics.

The objective of PR is to make a company, its brand(s), product(s), and/or service(s) look credible in the eyes of the public by generating free publicity through the media. Today, social media like Facebook and Twitter, company websites, news releases, feature articles, white papers, press conferences, event sponsorship, and employee relations play a key role in the execution of public relations strategies. Canada Goose reinforced its "Made in Canada" positioning through public relations, when in 2015 it opened its second manufacturing facility in Winnipeg Manitoba and created 350 new jobs in the community (Newswire.ca, 2015).

Sales Promotion

Sales promotion is a pull strategy that is frequently implemented in conjunction with an advertising campaign for a product which is new or one which may not be receiving a lot of attention. Sales promotions strategies encourage an immediate buying response from consumers and use various techniques like coupons, cash refunds, and contests. Canada Goose is in a unique position where it doesn't put its products on sale. "You can wait until Boxing Day, the first week of January or the last week of July, the price is the price and isn't going down." (Hulsman, 2013)

IMC Plan—Personal Selling

Unlike advertising, personal selling involves direct contact between the buyer and seller. It gives marketers and sales teams the opportunity to present the features and benefits of a product or service to a buyer as well as any sales offers, incentives, discounts, or promotions that may come with it. The personal touch and individualized communication in personal selling, allows the seller to tailor and tweak the offer to the customer's specific need and then assess "on the spot" the reaction of the buyer.

Direct Response

Direct response or direct and digital marketing is almost individually targeted and delivered directly to specific consumers, usually through the medium of their choice. Today's direct marketing goes beyond mail and telephone communication. New technology and innovations in mobile messaging, social media sites, and even home cable have made direct marketing more immediate and personalized. Messages are prepared almost on the spot and are delivered in real time to segments of the population, allowing marketers the chance to communicate with consumers and to record their reactions to their offers. Direct response also affords consumers the chance to be in the know within seconds and to decide if a product or service is right for them.

Practice...

1. How can a sales force utilize an IMC message?
   a. They can hand out free samples of the product in malls to let the people try the product out.
   b. They can focus on the same key promotional message that the advertising, sales promotion, and public relations elements contain.
   c. They can offer tremendous discounts on the price of the product in addition to promoting it.
   d. They can concentrate on the price of the product, and the demand from the end consumer.

2. A communication message is integrated when it _____.
   a. has the same spokesperson
   b. changes depending upon sales forecasts
   c. is the same even if it's from a television ad, magazine article, or social media site
   d. assesses and reacts to competitive threats

3. How would a new condominium development company implement IMC in their sales promotions?
   a. By stressing to their sales staff that they have to close the deal by using traditional techniques
   b. By designing a billboard that will be located on a busy commuter route
   c. By ensuring their street display ads have the same image and theme as their TV advertising
   d. By creating original and eye-catching transit display ads

4. The difference between personal selling and sales promotion is that:
   a. it involves direct contact between the buyer and seller.
   b. it uses using digital channels to reach consumers.
   c. it relies heavily on PR to close a sale.
   d. it uses all the advertising media to promote a message.

5. IMC is:
   a. not a stand-alone concept but rather one that requires a variety of tools.
   b. only requires a strong sales force to get the message across to consumers.
   c. necessary in order for a sponsorship deal to take place.
   d. reliant on advertising.

 # Apply...

1. Individually, consider the following: Would advertising be the right promotional tool to promote athletic trackers like Fitbit or the apple watch? Explain your rationale then get ready to present your reasoning to the class.

   _____

   _____

   _____

   _____

   _____

   _____

   _____

   _____

   _____

   _____

   _____

   _____

   _____

   _____

   _____

2. Individually, give an example of a company that uses sales promotion as part of their IMC strategy. Is this effective for all types of companies? Why or why not?

   _____

   _____

   _____

   _____

   _____

   _____

   _____

   _____

   _____

   _____

   _____

   _____

   _____

   _____

   _____

   _____

KNOW...

Learning Objectives

1. The core of a marketing plan is the marketing mix. The marketing mix consists of product, place, promotion, and price. The correct mix must be created by the marketer in order to communicate effectively with the target market and produce a sale.

2. In order to compete in today's difficult market, a marketing manager must create not just a promotional mix, but an integrated marketing communications plan. This is a coordinating plan of promotional messages for a product to ensure consistency. The product's promotional message should be consistent and create an overall integrated theme in order to make it easier for the consumer to purchase a product.

3. Marketers must decide on a strategy. Push promotion strategies push a product or service into the hands of consumers, while pull promotion strategies induce customers to pull a product from its producer.

4. After selecting a push or pull strategy, the marketer will decide on the tools that will shape their communication to consumers. They need to also recognize that with IMC, each of these tools is not a stand-alone discipline but rather, one of the pieces that will complement the consumer's decision-making process and ultimately drive sales. The tools include advertising, PR, sales promotion, personal selling, and direct response.

Key Terms

Direct Response: Direct and digital marketing that is individually targeted and delivered directly to specific consumers through their choice of medium.

Five Touch Points of the Promotional Part of the Marketing Mix: Advertising, public relations, personal selling, sales promotion, and direct response.

Integrated Marketing Communications (IMC): Integration of communication channels to deliver a clear, consistent, and compelling message about the organization and its brands.

Marketing Mix: The set of actions, or tactics, that a company uses to promote its brand or product in the market. In marketing, the 4P's make up a typical marketing mix.

Place: The distribution of the product and the availability of the service.

Price: Refers to the cost a customer must pay to obtain the product.

Product: Refers to what the company is offering the market.

Promotion: The activities that communicate the merits of the product or service and persuade consumers to purchase it.

4 P's of the Marketing Mix: Product, price, place, and promotion.

Pull Strategy: A promotion strategy that induces final consumers to buy the product, creating a demand vacuum that "pulls" the product through the channel.

Push Strategy: Pushing a product through marketing channels to final consumers.

Answers to Practice

Integrated Marketing Mix
1. c   2. b   3. b   4. a   5. d

Integrated Marketing Communications (IMC)
1. b   2. c   3. c   4. c   5. b

Promotion Strategies
1. a   2. c   3. a   4. c   5. d

Promotion Tools
1. b   2. c   3. c   4. a   5. a

References

Armstrong, Gary; Kotler, Philip, Marketing: An Introduction, 13th Ed., ©2017. Reprinted and Electronically reproduced by permission of Pearson Education, Inc., New York, NY.

Armstrong, Kotler, Trifts, Buchwitz, Marketing An Introduction, Pearson Canada, 2017.

Hulsman, N. (January 16, 2013). Why Canada Goose will never go on sale. *Yahoo Finance.* Retrieved from https://ca.finance.yahoo.com/blogs/insight/why-canada-goose-never-sale-171840302.html.

Keith Tuckwell, Canadian Advertising In Action, p.6, Pearson, 2015.

Newswire.ca, Canada Goose Bolsters 'Made In Canada' Commitment With Opening of Second Winnipeg Manufacturing Facility, 2015.

Retrieved from https://roots.com/on/demandware.store/Sites-RootsCorporate-Site/default/Page-Show?cid=MSTR_COMPANY_FACT_SHEET.

Singh, H. (September 15, 2016). Canada Goose keeps it out there. *Strategy Magazine.*

11 Marketing Information

LEARNING OBJECTIVES

LO1 Define what customer insights are and why they are important to marketing

LO2 Understand why MIS is important to marketing and how companies use them

LO3 Understand the role internal data plays in developing marketing information

LO4 Explain what marketing intelligence is and how it is used by marketers

LO5 Identify each part of a marketing research strategy

LEARN...

Today's consumers have changed dramatically in how they choose to work with their favourite companies and brands. They have different backgrounds, receive and process information differently, and interact with brands in different ways. In order to get ahead of their competition, marketers need to gain and apply information or *insights* on the customer and market they serve. Marketers that do not search for consumer insights will find it difficult to connect and motivate customers, as well as to compete with other companies.

As marketers, we are aware that we can no longer take the attitude of Henry Ford and give customers "any color of car. . ." that they want, ". . . so long as it's black". Companies have realized that in order to succeed they need to stay in touch with customers and offer them a wide variety of products, services, colors, and fashions, so that they can appeal to their ever-changing palette. Without gaining information or insights into customers, businesses will never be able to develop the products their customers want or to promote them in a way that gains attention.

In order to gain that information, marketers can use a variety of methods and tools such as internal databases, competitive marketing intelligence, and research, to gain an insight and to better understand customers and the environment they live in. This information should not only provide a current portrait of the marketing landscape but also insight into what direction a marketing strategy should take on. Therefore, more and better information will most likely equate to greater success. It will tell a company whether or not they are on the right track, as well as a sense of direction for the future.

Customer Insights

L01 Define what customer insights are and why they are important to marketing

Why do some products jump off the shelves while others languish in obscurity? Each company may assert that it has done in-depth market research but have they truly looked for consumer insights which would make their product more desirable?

In a study conducted by Lego in 2008, it was reported that *only 9% of the primary users of their toy were female*. Upon seeing this, the company decided to come out with a new product to entice more girls to play with Legos. They researched approximately 4,500 girls and then studied their playing habits.

At the conclusion of the research in 2014, Lego came out with a new line of toys called "*Friends*". The new product skewed girls, the Lego brick colors were more vibrant, the packaging changed, and figurines included in the set were made slightly bigger in order to accommodate accessories such as hairbrushes and purses that the figurines could grip. *Friends* was a smashing success. Since the line's debut, Lego's profits have averaged a 15% increase annually and the company has pulled in more than $5.4 billion in revenue—up 25% compared with 2014. Furthermore, the share of Lego toys bought for girls now represents "significantly more" of overall Lego sales in 2018 (LaFrance, 2016).

For Lego, there are three successes here: monetary gain, a new Friends product, and an untapped new target audience for their toy. All would not have been possible without **customer insights**. Better insight *will drive differentiation, give you a competitive advantage in the market, and a stronger return on your investment.*

Customer insights are defined as:

> *Fresh understandings of customers and the marketplace derived from marketing information that become the basis for creating customer value and relationships.* (Armstrong et al., 2017)

Today's marketer has realized the value of this information and are tapping into a variety of traditional and non-traditional sources. And unlike the past, today's insights are not only initiated by the marketer but are also initiated by the consumer. Emails, text messages, blogs, social media, chat forums, and other grass root channels are all important tools that marketers and customers are accessing for real time and fairly inexpensive marketing information.

Yet the abundance of information does not necessarily equate to better and more marketing communications campaigns. In a study conducted by the Economist Intelligence Unit, 48% of the companies interviewed felt that their organizations have failed to take advantage of opportunities to capitalize on the information (Marr, 2016).

Given the abundance of information sources available today, marketers don't necessarily need more information but strong insights about their customers that can be used to accomplish their objectives and better their campaigns.

Practice...

1. Marketers today don't necessarily need more information, they need:
   a. better information.
   b. more quantitative information.
   c. a greater return on their investment.
   d. a more secure process to gauge campaigns.

2. The fact that *only 9% of Lego were female* is a:
   a. statistic.
   b. research question.
   c. customer insight.
   d. observation.

3. The main objective of customer insights is to:
   a. boost sales.
   b. create customer value and relationship.
   c. boost visits to customer social media site.
   d. create a stronger rapport among internal employees.

4. Today's customer insights are initiated by:
   a. the marketer.
   b. the customer.
   c. technology.
   d. the marketer and customer.

5. Today customer insights are collected from:
   a. the company's annual report.
   b. the promotions of a company.
   c. internal staff.
   d. digital channels like social media, email, and blogs.

 **Apply...**

1. Individually, consider the following: McDonald's over the years has brought in different types of food products due to consumer insights and "gut feeling". Take a look at the timeline (https://tinyurl.com/flextext-mcdonalds) and types of foods offered by McDonald's over the years. Identifying several of the products why do you think some drop off while others become a staple for the company?

_____

_____

_____

_____

_____

_____

_____

_____

_____

_____

_____

_____

_____

_____

_____

_____

_____

2. Individually, answer the following: Choosing one of your favourite brands, what consumer insights can you provide to that organization to make the company's marketing create more demand? Analyze this from the perspective of the four P's. Present your insights to the class.

_____

_____

_____

_____

_____

_____

_____

_____

_____

_____

Marketing Information System (MIS)

L02 Understand why MIS is important to marketing and how companies use them

Companies need to know their market very well in order to compete and make informed decisions about their brands and products. Smarter companies today are developing teams whose sole purpose is to make sense of all the information that is collected from the market and to develop insights on the customer. These "need to know" versus "nice to know" insights will provide a clearer picture for marketers and allow them a chance to devise strategies that appeal to their customers.

As mentioned earlier, there is a lot of information out there. So companies have designed **marketing information system (MIS)** or **(MkIS)** that take all the data and information and translate it into customer knowledge that can then be used by management to make better marketing decisions and/or solve problems.

According to Armstrong et al. (2017),

> *a marketing information system consists of people and procedures dedicated to assessing information needs, developing the needed information and helping decision makers use the information to generate and validate actionable customer and market insights.*

When selecting a marketing information system, marketers look at the type of data and product information that can be tracked from a variety of external and internal sources at any instant or for a particular purpose. MIS is necessary and useful to today's marketer because they track usage and sentiment of new and existing brands, products, and innovations in the market.

MIS begins at the user level, that is, the marketing managers and other stakeholders, because it is important to understand the needs and the goals of the information user. Once needs are clarified, information is collected almost on a daily basis from a variety of internal and external sources including:

- internal databases,
- marketing intelligence, and
- marketing research.

Once all the information is "mined", it is analyzed into customer insights and presented back to the marketing managers and stakeholders, who then assess the current strategy and react and/or respond with similar or better future customer campaigns. The power of computing and technology has caused a rapid evolution of software which allows the marketer to gather information from a variety of sources and then store and analyze it more quickly than ever before. Most analysis today is provided in real time, which allows managers access to the most recent information and a chance to respond and make decisions quickly (Figure 1).

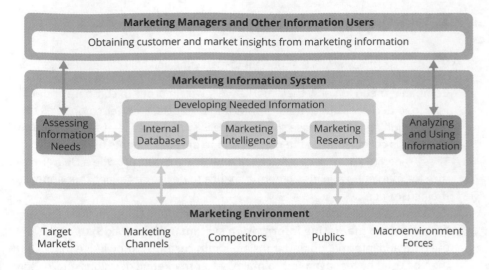

FIGURE 1 The marketing information system. A Marketing Information System (MIS) first assesses the needs of the marketing manager and then the internal and external environment, before coming up with key customer insights that aid with strategy.

Source: Pearson Education Inc.

Practice...

1. Which of the following is not a way to collect data for a marketing information system?
   a. Provide customers with a discount card they can carry on their key rings.
   b. Ask in-store customers to visit the website address printed on their receipts.
   c. Ask customers to take online surveys.
   d. Produce a new online app for a product.

2. What is a consideration that must be made when selecting a marketing information system?
   a. The education level of your customers
   b. The type of data and product information that is needed
   c. The marketability of the product
   d. The state of the stock market

3. What is a marketing information system?
   a. A smartphone app that helps consumers to compare while shopping for products.
   b. A program focused on the youth market that compares product features and helps a company to rank their products with shoppers between the ages of 13 and 18 years.
   c. A software application that helps a company to analyze marketing data, customer information, and competitor data.
   d. A system that focuses solely on historic marketing activities and results.

4. What is another name for a marketing information system?
   a. MkIS
   b. MDD
   c. Data Analyzer
   d. Marketing Data Information Source

5. What of these is not a benefits of a marketing information system?
   a. It helps you understand what motivates people to buy a product.
   b. It provides you with information about your customers' buying habits and wants.
   c. It helps you to know more about your competitors' actions.
   d. It provides information to upper management on employee morale and satisfaction.

 Apply...

1. In groups of four, present your findings to the class. If you were developing a new loyalty program using an MIS for H&M (http://www2.hm.com/en_ca/index.html), what type of data and product information would you require your MIS to track?

_____

_____

_____

_____

_____

_____

_____

_____

_____

_____

_____

_____

_____

2. In groups of four, present your findings to the class. Do some research online and provide a brief overview on how Walmart has incorporated MIS into their strategic marketing (and planning). Use the key phrase "Walmart history of MIS" to help you.

_____

_____

_____

_____

_____

_____

_____

_____

_____

_____

_____

_____

_____

Developing Marketing Information with Internal Data

L03 Understand the role internal data plays in developing marketing information

Every company has an internal network that sends and receives data from various sources within and outside the company. That internal network has the ability to collect and store information like sales data, competitor activities, consumer feedback, etc., into a database.

Internal databases are:

electronic collections of consumer and market information obtained from data sources within the company network.
(Armstrong et al., 2017)

The internal database is an important component of the Marketing Information System, because it provides marketers quick access to all types of information without having to use an external (and more expensive) source. It also brings together and informs internal management on the progress of the strategies they are currently using and if shifts need to be made.

There are five different areas from where a company can gather internal data from. They are:

- Marketing
- Sales
- Customer service
- Accounting
- Operations

Each area provides a unique perspective that can help with marketing strategy.

Marketing

There are countless ways to track marketing efforts. Unlike other areas of the company where reports are necessary, some businesses do not even realize the opportunities technology provides in the area of marketing. Internal data can be gathered from a variety of sources like website traffic statistics, phone reports, in-store promotion codes, or social media contests. This information can immediately be sourced back to marketing information system and tweaks, if necessary, can be made.

For example, a clothing company is running a campaign in partnership with a charity. The charity promotes a code to its Instagram followers to type in when they checkout on the clothing company's website to receive an additional 20% off. The clothing company can track the number of people who used the code to determine the success of the campaign. In this instance, the internal marketing data can help the company to determine if future campaigns of this type would be successful.

Sales

Internal data is gathered from the sales department to determine revenue, profit, and the bottom line. It also provides information and reasoning to place more focus on particular areas or cut them out altogether. Sales numbers can be broken down further by analyzing the progress and reactions of the salesperson, the reseller, distribution channel, competitor, price point, geographic area, and customer type.

For example, a lawn care company is running a special to have lawns mowed at 50% off if the customer signs a contract in the month of April. As the company breaks down the sales by geographic area, it is determined that this campaign is highly successful on the north side of the city, yet failing on the south side. This internal data tells the company to continue this campaign where it is successful and make adjustments to try to improve sales on the south side. In addition, the company should review the salesperson data to see if the issue is a lack of employee training or a geographical issue prior to making the change.

Accounting

The accounting department should be providing detailed sales, cost, and cash flow report. Accounting data conveys how much goes in and out of the company on a monthly basis as well as the days these transactions occur. This tells management when the best times to order supplies are, and it helps the cost per unit. Keeping the cost down allows the company to price properly and keep profit margins at the necessary level.

Operations

Operations focus on designing and controlling the process of production, shipments, and inventories and help the marketing team to achieve their goals by manufacturing products that revolve around the customer's needs and then distributing those products to the customer.

Customer Service

The customer service department reports and tracks all positive and negative customer experiences. For example, customer service can notify marketing of instances when inadequate or misleading expectations have been set. The marketer then will be able to modify the campaign(s) to better set expectations for potential customers.

Practice...

1. What is internal data?
    a. Data retrieved from inside the company to make decisions for successful operations.
    b. Data that distinguishes why there is conflict within a group.
    c. Data from the competition.
    d. Data retrieved from outside the company to make decisions for successful operations.

2. What type of internal data does the accounting department supply?
    a. Sales, finance, marketing, and human resources
    b. Cash flow, reports, and sales reports
    c. Website traffic statistics, phone reports, and promotion codes
    d. Rates of retention, tardiness, payroll, and absenteeism

3. What areas of a company supply internal data?
    a. Marketing, operations, and accounting
    b. Sales, accounting, marketing, customer service, and operations
    c. Marketing and customer relations
    d. Sales and accounting

4. What type of internal data does the marketing department supply?
    a. Website traffic statistics, phone reports, and promotion codes
    b. Rates of retention, tardiness, payroll, and absenteeism
    c. Cash flow reports, production reports, and a budget variance analysis
    d. Sales, finance, marketing, and human resources

5. What type of internal data does the operations department supply?
    a. Production, shipment, and inventory reports
    b. Cash flow reports, production reports, and a budget variance analysis
    c. Rates of retention, tardiness, payroll, and absenteeism
    d. Sales, finance, marketing, and human resources

 **Apply...**

1. In groups of four, present your findings to the class. You are the owner of a car dealership in town, and have noticed that people are not responding to a $1,000 off promotion that you are running on radio. From the five internal areas identified above, which of these need to be asked to attend a sales meeting to try to figure out why the promotion isn't working. Support your choices. Present your answers to the class.

_____

_____

_____

_____

_____

_____

_____

_____

_____

_____

_____

_____

_____

2. In groups of four, present your findings to the class. You have just opened a second sporting goods store in your community (opposite side of the community) and would like to increase awareness and sales at this new store. What marketing tactics (mediums) would you use that would allow you to track and monitor information for your internal database? Present your marketing ideas to the class.

_____

_____

_____

_____

_____

_____

_____

_____

_____

_____

_____

_____

_____

_____

Developing Marketing Information with Marketing Intelligence

LO4 Explain what marketing intelligence is and how it is used by marketers

Companies need to know their market very well in order to make informed decisions about their brands and products. They need to know about the general everyday information and circumstances that may impact and affect their business, market, products, and services and even competitors.

Let's suppose you are the owner of a new restaurant in town. Your restaurant does a brisk business but as a *smart* businessperson, you need to stay on top of things and know what is going on in the market, who your competitors are, who your customers are, and what people think about your food and service. You decide to gather marketing information from a variety of sources—internal and external—to find out what is happening in the market and to store it in the MIS for future use. The more insights you have, the better your ideas and strategies will be on who, when, where, and how to reach your audience. This intelligent action on your behalf to collect marketing information about your market, customer, and competitor, should help to set you aside from the other restaurants in the community and position you for success.

Marketing intelligence is,

> *the systematic collection and analysis of publicly available information about consumers, competitors and developments in the marketing environment.* (Armstrong et al., 2017)

Armstrong further states that the goal of competitive marketing intelligence is to improve strategic decision making by:

- understanding the consumer environment,
- assessing and tracking competitor's actions, and
- providing early warning of opportunities and threats.

Good marketing intelligence is collected daily through a variety of means and it helps companies to understand everyday information in the market. The information comes into the MIS through a variety of ways that can include— customer service centres, frontline staff, social media, and even word of mouth and can be sourced back to company staff or even consumers who are followers of your brand. The information received at the end of the day, prepares businesses and marketers in specific, for decision making that will help to define and shape the marketing strategy of a company.

Most companies start their marketing intelligence by tracking their current customers and looking at their purchases and experiences with their brand or other similar brands. They can solicit customer feedback through personal interviews with their customers, or by using social media channels like Facebook, Twitter, or blogs, to get a feel of what customers feel or think about them or any new competitors or entries to the market. This customer feedback helps companies to carry on or modify their strategy where necessary and provide better service and products to their loyal customers.

After a company gathers everyday information on its customers, the next type of market intelligence it will most likely seek is that of its competitors. Companies need to know how many competitors are in their market for the same products and services and what they do to differentiate and give them an advantage. For example, if you as a restaurant owner know that your customers were active in the mobile market and that your competitors were introducing new products and special offers to customers with mobile devices, you may need to up your mobile product offering to keep up with the competition and devote more resources to mobile market products.

Marketing intelligence can also be used to leverage market opportunities. For example, let's say you gathered information on your competitors from online and social media forums and found that your competitor's customers are dissatisfied with the over an hour delivery time for meals. This insight allows you to address an opportunity for your restaurant and can come up with an "under 30 minute or its free" marketing campaign to take advantage of your competitor's flaw.

At the end of the day, all this information is brought to the MIS, deciphered and presented as insights to the marketing team.

Practice...

1. Which is a situation where marketing intelligence was used?
   a. You open a new restaurant in town without doing research.
   b. You expand your restaurant operations into a new market because it seems like a good idea.
   c. You expand your restaurant operations and use customer information before launching it.
   d. You decide to lay off restaurant employees to save money after analyzing production methods.

2. When possible, how often should marketing intelligence be collected?
   a. Daily
   b. Weekly
   c. Monthly
   d. Every quarter

3. Which is not an example of a company's use of marketing intelligence?
   a. Marketing intelligence can be used for decision making.
   b. Marketing intelligence can be used for market strategy.
   c. Marketing intelligence can be used for setting goals.
   d. Marketing intelligence can be used to decide which company employees to fire.

4. What is marketing intelligence?
   a. Sending in a spy to gain competitor information
   b. Collecting and evaluating information about a company's market
   c. Distributing intelligence about products
   d. The knowledge of the company's workforce

5. What is an example of everyday information used in marketing intelligence?
   a. Employee feedback
   b. Competitor P & L statements
   c. Customer feedback
   d. Shareholder feedback

 **Apply...**

1. In groups of two, answer the following: As the marketing co-ordinator for the mountain bike company Trek (https://www.trekbikes.com/ca/en_CA/?clear=true), you have been asked to open a new retail mountain bike shop in southern Alberta. You have several communities to choose from including Lethbridge, Taber, Medicine Hat, and High River. What type of marketing would you need to collect before opening your store? Present your answers to the class.

_____
_____
_____
_____
_____
_____
_____
_____
_____
_____
_____
_____
_____
_____
_____
_____
_____
_____
_____
_____
_____
_____
_____
_____
_____
_____
_____

to be continued

 **Apply…**

continued

2. In groups of two, consider the following: Once opened, what type of marketing intelligence would you conduct to monitor the success of your new location? Present your answers to class.

_____

_____

_____

_____

_____

_____

_____

_____

_____

_____

_____

_____

_____

_____

_____

_____

_____

_____

_____

_____

_____

_____

_____

_____

_____

_____

_____

_____

_____

_____

Developing Marketing Information Through Marketing Research

 Identify each part of a marketing research strategy

Topic content

In addition to internal databases and marketing intelligence, marketers need more formal studies to assess the effectiveness of their specific campaigns and strategies and to find out or *research* if the various aspects of the marketing mix that they have employed are effective.

Marketing research is,

> *the systematic design, collection, analysis and reporting of data relevant to a specific marketing situation facing an organization.* (Armstrong, 2017)

It's an examination conducted by the marketer to find out if their decisions and marketing mix efforts work.

What Is Marketing Research Used For?

Marketing research can be used to track a variety of things, including:

- customer purchase behaviour
- customer motivations
- customer satisfaction
- brand or product market share
- the effectiveness of a 4P marketing mix
- the quality of decision making
- the tracking of problems that may exist in the marketing process
    - ◊ (that is, targeting, media, messaging, or distribution)
- finding ways to keep existing clients loyal
- finding ways to increase purchase behaviour
- understanding trends and environmental changes
    - ◊ (that is, online purchasing or social and mobile media preferences)

Research can be obtained in a variety of ways. Some companies conduct their own "in house" research, with dedicated research teams working hand in hand with the marketing team. Some use the services of an external marketing research specialist to conduct research on the marketer's behalf. Some marketers also boost their customer insights by purchasing information collected from third-party companies to aid in their decision making.

The Process

The marketing process has four steps: problem definition, research design and information gathering, collecting and analyzing data, and preparing and presenting information (Figure 2).

Problem Solving and Objectives

The first step (and probably hardest) is to figure out the problem and come up with objectives that will guide the research process. A marketing research project can have one of three objectives:

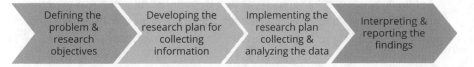

FIGURE 2 The marketing research process.

Source: Based on "The Marketing Research Process", Armstrong et al.

- Exploratory
  - ◊ Preliminary information that will help to define the problem and suggest hypotheses
- Descriptive
  - ◊ Information that describes characteristics of a population or phenomenon being studied, like attitudes or market potential
- Causal
  - ◊ Investigating the effect of one variable on another, like the increase in television advertising parlaying into an increase in product sales

Once the problem has been identified, marketers need to decide if primary or secondary data will be required to solve the problem.

Data Collection

Secondary data is data previously collected for any purpose other than the one at hand. This data is for the most part free and includes proprietary data such as sales receipts, invoices, and non-proprietary data such as competitive information, online consumer information, and economic trends. Because this information is easily accessible, it saves the researcher's both time and money and a solution to the problem can be easily and quickly reached.

Primary data is information that is collected for the first time and used for the purpose of solving the research problem and objective. The biggest issue with primary data is that it is very expensive because the researcher is conducting his or her own research from scratch. Primary data can be obtained through *survey research* where a researcher gathers descriptive information by interacting with people to obtain facts, opinions, and attitudes. Surveys can be:

- Open-ended
  - ◊ The interview question encourages a long and descriptive answer phrased in the respondent's own words.
- Closed-ended
  - ◊ Respondents have to choose from a limited list of responses such as "yes" or "no".
- Scaled-response
  - ◊ A closed-ended *"1 to 5" or "Strongly Agree to Strongly Disagree"* question which measures the intensity of a respondent's answer

Primary data can also be obtained through **observational research** by observing the immediate environment and the interactions of the target audience with the brand, product, or service. This can be done via **ethnography**, by studying and observing consumers in its natural context such as a physical retail location or setting (that is, mystery shoppers or trained researchers who observe behaviour and attitudes in store) or through **netnography**, which observes consumers' behaviour in their natural context on the internet, blog, or social networks channels (Armstrong et al., 2017, p. 166).

Finally primary data can be collected by conducting a detailed experiment where marketers and researchers alter one or more of the 4P variables (price) while observing the effects on another variable (usually sales).

Collecting and Analyzing the Data

Data can be collected from respondents by the marketer's research team or by external field service firms that are hired by the marketer. Once collected, the data needs to be processed and analyzed to see if there is an important relationship that corresponds to the research problem and objective. Many times, data can be very rich and even confusing. As a result, companies and marketing organizations have turned to Customer Relationship Management (CRM) software analytical tools like SAS, Oracle, or Microsoft that integrate, analyze, and interpret the collected data into valuable solutions that build relationships with existing and potential customers.

Interpreting and Reporting the Findings

The last of the market research process is to present the research findings and come up with insights and recommendations that may help to rectify the problem at hand. These insights may be stored in the company's MIS and accessed by key marketing and business stakeholders for information that caters to their needs.

 # Practice...

1. The study of the human behaviour in its natural context is an example of _____.
   a. survey research
   b. experimental research
   c. ethnographic research
   d. focus groups

2. Which of the following is an example of a closed-ended question?
   a. Why do you shop at Bob's Sub sandwich shop?
   b. Is Bob's Subs your favourite place to eat?
   c. Could you describe your favourite Bob's Sub sandwich?
   d. What toppings do you like with your sub?

3. Which one of the following scenarios do not represent a marketing research study?
   a. A survey is conducted in a theme park to discover why attendance has dropped.
   b. A focus group is held for a local soup manufacturer to decide what flavours they should develop.
   c. Doctors are interviewed about whether a new facial plastic surgery tool would work for surgery.
   d. A manager has to decide which company employee should receive a raise.

4. What is an advantage of using primary data instead of secondary data?
   a. The data has already been collected, so it can be examined immediately.
   b. It relies on statistical data and is therefore more reliable.
   c. It is less expensive and more efficient to collect and analyze.
   d. The research design can be tailored to address specific questions.

5. Which of the following would be considered secondary data collection?
   a. Bringing in a focus group to get its opinion on a new product
   b. Examining information such as competitor price offerings
   c. Creating a survey to determine customer satisfaction
   d. Observing the outcomes of customer-salesperson interactions

Developing Marketing Information Through Marketing Research **217**

 **Apply...**

1. In pairs, answer the following. What type of secondary data sources would you use to predict the success of the new mountain bike shop you want to open in Southern Alberta? What primary sources would you consider employing? Present your answers to the class.

_____

_____

_____

_____

_____

_____

_____

_____

_____

_____

_____

_____

_____

_____

_____

_____

_____

2. In pairs, go online and find an example of a company which uses ethnography to better understand how their consumers think. What type of environment were the respondents studied in? Find a company that uses netnography to better understand their consumers. What social media sites did the company track?

_____

_____

_____

_____

_____

_____

_____

_____

_____

_____

_____

_____

_____

_____

KNOW...

Learning Objectives

1. Given the abundance of information sources available today, marketers don't necessarily need more information but better information that provides an insight into their customers. Marketers tap into a variety of traditional and non-traditional sources like emails, text messages, blogs, and social media and chat forums to access this "real time" and inexpensive information.

2. A marketing information system (MIS) is a software program that collects and evaluates information that can be used to make both business and marketing decisions. The information provided by an MIS can help you to determine what your customers want, what their buying habits are, and the best way to market products to them. Additionally, an MIS can help you understand what your competitors are doing and plan accordingly.

3. Running a business takes a lot of information! Once a company is up and running, it needs every bit of internal data it can get its hands on to make the right decisions. Internal data is data retrieved from inside the company to make decisions for successful operations. There are five different areas a company can gather internal data from: sales, accounting, marketing, operations, and customer service. Internal sales data is collected to determine revenue, profit, and the bottom line. The accounting department supplies sales, cost, and cash flow reports. Internal marketing data can be gathered from website traffic statistics, phone reports, promotion codes, etc. Operations reports on production, shipments, and inventories. Customer service department keeps track of customer satisfaction or service problems. All this data is stored in a database and is a vital component of a company's MIS.

4. Companies need information about their customers, competitors, and their market. Marketing intelligence is when a company collects and uses information pertaining to its market. Everyday information about customers and competitors is vital for the running of a company on a daily basis. Marketing intelligence can also be used for decision making and defining market strategy.

5. Marketing research is the process of planning, collecting, and analyzing data relevant to a marketing decision. There are valuable ways that marketing research can help businesses. The steps in the marketing research process are to identify the problem, plan a research design, collect data, analyze data, prepare, and present the report, and follow-up.

Key Terms

Customer Insights: The attempt to discover truth about consumers, their aspirations, and motivations which can in turn be used to generate customer value, relationships, and business growth.

Ethnography: Studying and observing consumers in their physical location or setting (that is, mystery shoppers or trained researchers who may observe customer behaviour and attitudes in store).

Internal Database: A collection of information on current and prospective customers that may include demographic data, psychographic data, purchase history, and a record of types and frequencies of interactions with the brand.

Marketing Information System (MIS): A management information system or MIS is a set of procedures and methods for the regular, planned collection, analysis, and presentation of information for use in making management decisions.

Marketing Intelligence: The gathering of data and information about all aspects of consumers' and competitors' marketing and business activities for the purposes of formulating plans and strategies and making decisions.

Marketing Research: The collection, analysis, design, and reporting of data relevant to a specific marketing situation, customers, consumers and/or competitors facing an organization.

Netnography: Observes consumers in their natural context on the internet, blog, or social networks channels.

Observational Research: Observing the immediate environment and the interactions of the target audience with the brand, product, or service.

Primary Data: Information that is collected for the first time and used for the purpose of solving the research problem and objective.

Secondary Data: Data previously collected for any purpose other than the marketing research project at hand. This data is for the most part free and includes proprietary data such as sales receipts, invoices, and non-proprietary data such as competitive information, online consumer information, and economic trends.

Answers to Practice

Customer Insights
1. a   2. c   3. b   4. d   5. d

Marketing Information System (MIS)
1. d   2. b   3. c   4. a   5. d

Developing Marketing Information with Internal Data
1. a   2. b   3. b   4. a   5. a

Developing Marketing Information with Marketing Intelligence
1. c   2. a   3. d   4. b   5. c

Developing Marketing Information Through Marketing Research
1. c   2. b   3. d   4. d   5. b

References

Armstrong, Gary; Kotler, Philip, Marketing: An Introduction, 13th Ed., ©2017. Reprinted and Electronically reproduced by permission of Pearson Education, Inc., New York, NY.

Armstrong, Kotler, Trifts, Buchwitz. (2017). *Marketing, An Introduction*. Pearson.

LaFrance, A. (May 25, 2016). How to play like a girl. *The Atlantic*. Retrieved from https://www.theatlantic.com/entertainment/archive/2016/05/legos/484115/.

Marr, B. (January 13, 2016). Big data facts: How many companies are really making money from their data? *Forbes*. Retrieved from https://www.forbes.com/sites/bernardmarr/2016/01/13/big-data-60-of-companies-are-making-money-from-it-are-you/#3c0e07382d8f.

Ethics and Marketing

LEARNING OBJECTIVES

 LO1 Explain the role of ethics in business

LO2 Define ethics, laws, mores, and levels of ethical development

LO3 Define the meaning of ethical marketing

LO4 Identify some of the types of unethical marketing used by marketers

LEARN...

A survey released by the Ethics Resource Center in 2012, found that 42% of respondents believed that their supervisors lacked ethical integrity (Ethics Resource Center, 2011).

With the tightening of budgets and the increased scrutiny of companies by consumers even their employees, the relationship between doing the ethical or "right thing" and making money has been a touchy and complicated subject.

Companies today have come to realize the importance of acting in a more ethical way and have created guidelines and policies specifically addressing marketing and how it deals with external partners and distributors, pricing policies, advertising standards, customer service, and product development. Following strict ethical rules should alleviate any negative perception in the marketplace and provide a company—through the marketer—a forum to communicate to customers and the general public on their actions.

Making use of the marketing channels is a proactive opportunity for a company to promote its ethical conduct and will reflect positively on every area of its business including its profile, reputation, relationship with consumers and ultimately, profitability. Marketers should also be aware that unethical marketing can harm customers, society, and eventually a company's brand and reputation.

Ethics and Business

 LO1 Explain the role of ethics in business

LO2 Define ethics, laws, mores, and levels of ethical development

Your company has just introduced a fat-free granola bar that contains olestra—a fat substitute that adds no fat, calories, or cholesterol to products. A few years ago, the FDA ruled that when consumed, olestra may affect the gastrointestinal system of consumers. This is your first marketing assignment with the company and you are stuck between a rock and a hard place. Do you market the product and make an impression with upper management or do you resist?

At the end you resist. But what was it that prevented you from marketing the product? The answer to your resistance is that it is, usually, your ethics that prevented you from marketing the granola to the market.

Ethics are defined as (American Marketing Association):

> *the moral principles (or values) that govern a person's behaviour or the conducting of an activity.*

Business ethics determine companies' everyday conduct. They are important because companies must follow—written and many times unwritten—rules to protect the environment, customers, and their reputation. Many times, these rules are mandated by management and employees but more so, these rules are the mandate of the consumer. According to the Deloitte Millennial Survey 2017, 73% of millennials believe that businesses should make a positive impact on their community and the world at large and see business as a broadly positive force that behaves in an increasingly responsible way (The Deloitte Millennial Survey, 2017).

Business ethics include both laws and mores, which ultimately determine how an employee will act in the business world.

Laws define the boundaries of what is legal and are the written guidelines that must be followed in society (American Marketing Association).

In the case of our trail mix bar example, what are the legalities of promoting and selling a product that contains olestra? Are there laws that protect consumers from the harmful side effects of this substitute? If yes, it may limit and possibly forbid the marketer to market the product.

Mores are the rules or parameters that people develop as a result of cultural norms and values. Mores are traditionally learned from childhood, culture, education, religion, etc. and are differentiated as either good or bad behaviour. Mores are defined as:

> *the cultural norms that specify behavio[u]r of vital importance to society and embody its basic moral values. The prohibition against bigamy or child abandonment in some cultures are examples. Mores often are codified into law such that legal as well as social sanctions can be applied to assure conformity.* (American Marketing Association)

In the case of our trail mix bar, would a marketer who fully understands that the product could make them sick, have good mores if they pushed olestra trail mix on a customer?

Psychologist Lawrence Kohlberg identified three levels of ethical development that individuals typically progress through.

1. Pre-conventional morality:

   Business and employees at this level are very self-centered and only driven by rewards or punishment. They usually would not consider implications or repercussions of their decisions.

2. Conventional morality:

   Business and employees *behave according to society's rules and expectations*. A marketing manager breaking a law in this case would be concerned more so about how the repercussion or actions would be viewed by outsiders and their peers.

3. Post-conventional morality:

    Revolves around the idea that people are more concerned about behaving correctly and how they view themselves and not what others may think. A marketing manager who has reached a level of post-conventional morality would not just consider the legal ramifications of a decision, but also how it could possibly hurt the environment or potentially, the customer (Bhardwaj, 2017).

    All three stages of ethical development can be applied to business and they allow us to assess not only the ethics but the motivation and soul of an organization and its employees and how they want to be regarded in the market.

    Many companies today manage ethics by offering corporate ethical training and guidelines that inform employees what is acceptable by employees and what they deem as ethical.

Practice...

1. What are the three levels of ethical development?
    a. Pan-conventional, conventional, neo-conventional
    b. Pre-conventional, conventional, post-conventional
    c. Post-conventional, pre-conventional, ple-conventional
    d. Post-conventional, conventional, morality

2. What are mores?
    a. The suggestions that govern the conduct of people
    b. The rules people develop as a result of cultural norms and values
    c. The courts and police
    d. The behaviour of employees towards their colleagues

3. How do companies manage ethics in the business world?
    a. They just let employees follow their instincts.
    b. They provide corporate ethical training and offer guidelines.
    c. They let outside agencies monitor them.
    d. They hope that employees have good morals.

4. What is the definition of ethics?
    a. The moral principles or values that generally govern the conduct of a group or individual.
    b. The rules people follow.
    c. The way companies keep their employees in line.
    d. The courts and police.

5. What is described as good or bad behaviour?
    a. Rules
    b. Laws
    c. Norms
    d. Mores

 # Apply...

1. In groups of four, present your findings to the class. Nike has been known for a number of unethical business practices over the past 25 years. How have they cleaned their act up? Click on the following link to learn more about some of the issues they have had and how they are trying to make it better: https://tinyurl.com/flextext-nike.

_____

_____

_____

_____

_____

_____

_____

_____

_____

_____

_____

_____

_____

2. In groups of four, present your findings to the class. Volkswagen has been in a heap of trouble over the past 24 months due to their installation of a piece of software dubbed the "defeat device". Haven't heard about it yet? Click on the following link to learn more about their unethical behaviour: https://tinyurl.com/flextext-vw. Which of the three types of moralities did Volkswagen employees used to make the decision to install the "defeat device"? Do you think it was a wise decision to implement this type of strategy? Explain.

_____

_____

_____

_____

_____

_____

_____

_____

_____

_____

_____

Ethics and Marketing

L03 Define the meaning of ethical marketing

Balancing ethics and remaining competitive can be difficult and there are many factors that companies consider when determining what the most ethical decision will be such as:

- The length of time between the decision and consequence
- The size of the consequence
- The probability of the consequence occurring
- The number of people that could be affected

All are considerations in determining an ethical path for businesses.

When it comes to conducting business most, if not all companies, would like to be viewed as ethical and as "doing the right thing". But it's hard for a company to assess if their decisions are ethical and if their efforts are perceived as ethical.

Most consumers approach marketing with a healthy degree of skepticism. Even the least informed consumer knows that not every claim made by every advertiser is true. The Figure 1 compiled from data from a Gallup Poll in 2016, shows just how skeptical consumers really are of marketers and advertisers. The study went on to say that fewer than 20% of respondents believed in advertising even most of the time.

It is clear that consumers have become cynical about the ads they see.

Being ethical when practicing marketing can be an effective way to restore some of the trust that has been lost between consumers and advertisers. It's something that is more and more demanded by consumers, as well by corporate management. According to an article in the Guardian, marketers are now taking up the torch to reflect this consumer and corporate view (MacLellan, December 10, 2015):

> *. . . the good news is that principled marketing professionals are now peeking above the parapet and it's starting to show. It's not only their ethics talking, it's because consumers are responding. Millennials in particular are demanding that businesses take on the bigger issues like climate change, social equality and animal rights.*

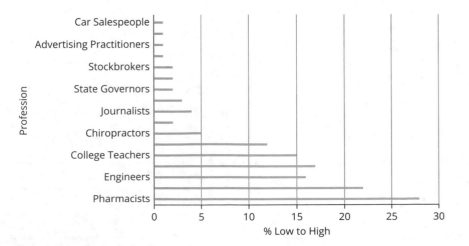

FIGURE 1 Consumer view of honesty/ethics in professions, December 2016.

Source: Pearson Education.

The Role of Ethics in Marketing

The Financial Times, defines **ethical marketing** as (Financial Times, 2017):

> *a process through which companies generate customer interest in products/services, build strong customer interest/relationships, and create value for all stakeholders by incorporating social and environmental considerations in products and promotions. All aspects of marketing are considered, from sales techniques to business communication and business development.*

Ethical marketing is about companies making marketing decisions and strategies that are morally right and valuable for their customers. The morality of the decision can encompass any part of the marketing process including the sourcing of raw materials, the employment of staff, and the promotion and pricing of products. But because everyone has subjective judgments about what is "right" and what is "wrong", ethical marketing is more of a philosophy than a strategy. There are no fixed rules but a general set of guidelines that seek to promote honesty, fairness, and responsibility in the 4P's of marketing.

Being an ethical marketer can help to:

- promote a company,

- improve a company's image, and

- develop trust and long-term relationships with customers and its many product offerings.

Balancing ethics and remaining competitive can be difficult. If ethical marketing involves considering the needs and welfare of suppliers, employees, and customers, it could also add to business costs. For example "Fair Trade" products provide producers with a respectable minimum wage price. By being Fair Trade, most times business costs increase and profit margins decrease and in many cases the costs are passed on to customers through price increases. However, if firms can adapt and communicate an ethical marketing platform which reflects the expectations of consumers, it may make them more appealing to customers and create a competitive advantage for the brand.

Ikea is one brand, whose corporate responsibility and product innovation processes are driven by ethics and sustainability commitments. Seventy-six percent of the cotton that it uses comes from sustainable sources, more than 700,000 solar panels have been installed on Ikea buildings worldwide and the group is committed to owning and operating 224 wind turbines.

This all has come together as a direct result of consumer influence and a change in corporate values. According to Magnus Holst, global manager of the Ikea Family loyalty scheme (Akhtar, 2015),

> *. . . consumers have a much wider view on brands today . . . and actively choose brands they want to be identified with, regardless of their product or service offer . . . Trust can only be earned by meeting consumer expectations and this includes a great product or service offer that aligns with inspiring and honest communication.*

Practice...

1. Ikea's decision to source most of its cotton from sustainable sources, came as a direct result of:
   a. the need to make a greater return on investment.
   b. consumer influence and a shift in corporate values.
   c. a supplier charging them higher prices than expected.
   d. a customer who had an allergic reaction to Ikea's cotton products.

2. The factor(s) that companies consider when making an ethical decision include:
   a. the length of time between the decision and consequence, the size of the consequence, the probability of the consequence occurring, and the number of people that could be affected.
   b. the size of the organization, the cost, and the time it takes to prepare a campaign.
   c. the media, the public feedback, and time of the campaign.
   d. the product, the price, place, and promotion being used.

3. Being an ethical marketer will most likely lead to:
   a. greater financial returns.
   b. better PR and an improvement of a company's image.
   c. more product offerings.
   d. increased competition.

4. Being ethical and taking on a corporate Fair Trade platform will most likely:
   a. increase the cost of doing business.
   b. decrease the cost of doing business.
   c. see an increase in profit margins.
   d. see an increase in competition.

5. Ethical marketing is more of a _____ that a company takes on.
   a. strategy
   b. mission
   c. vision
   d. philosophy

Apply...

1. In groups of four, present your findings to the class. Do magazine companies have a right to Photoshop models for their covers and images inside their magazine? What impact (if any) does this have on consumers? To learn more about this issue go to: https://tinyurl.com/flextext-photoshop. Are these tactics ethical? Explain.

    _____

    _____

    _____

    _____

    _____

    _____

    _____

    _____

    _____

    _____

    _____

    _____

2. In groups of four, present your findings to the class. Air Jordan Nike shoes are manufactured for around $16.00 USD.

    (https://tinyurl.com/flextext-sneakers). The question is should Nike be selling these shoes for up to $500.00 a pair? Did you know that kids are actually killed over these shoes (https://tinyurl.com/flextext-killed)? Is Nike obligated to do anything about it? Explain.

    _____

    _____

    _____

    _____

    _____

    _____

    _____

    _____

    _____

    _____

    _____

Types of Unethical Marketing and Policies to Protect Unethical Marketing

LO4 Identify some of the types of unethical marketing used by marketers

Identify the purpose of the Canadian Marketing Association and some of its policies.

According to the Canadian Marketing Association (2017),

> *Marketers are responsible for the content of their marketing communications and the practices of their suppliers and advertising agencies when in the course of executing marketing communications on their behalf.*

Based on this, every business has the opportunity to engage in ethical marketing. From the smallest mom and pop shop to the biggest multinational corporation, they all can choose to be ethical, open, honest, and fair when they market to their customers.

While it is impossible to claim that any company is completely ethical, marketing yourself as being ethical and responsible can be both profitable and effective. Companies that are known for treating workers fairly, sourcing sustainable materials, environmental stewardship, and charitable donation, usually reflect these principles in their marketing and communications efforts.

If a product lives up to the claims made in its marketing, it reflects positively on the entire company. It can make the consumer feel like the company is invested in the quality of the products and the value they provide to customers.

If it doesn't, the company may be penalized and consumer opinion may sway. Some categories and types of unethical marketing include (http://www.marketing-schools.org/types-of-marketing/ethical-marketing.html):

- **Surrogate Advertising**

  ◊ In certain places, there are laws against advertising products like cigarettes or alcohol. Surrogate advertising finds ways to remind consumers of these products without referencing them directly.

- **Exaggeration**

  ◊ Some advertisers use false claims about a product's quality or popularity. A Slogan like "get coverage everywhere on earth" advertises features that cannot be delivered.

  ◊ For example, Reebok paid $25 million in 2011 to settle charges over claims that their "toning shoes" could strengthen muscles in the legs, thighs, and buttocks. Ads even featured women in shorts with shapely bottoms and even claimed the shoes would "make your boobs jealous" (CBC News, 2012).

- **Puffery**

  ◊ When an advertiser relies on subjective rather than objective claims, they are puffing up their products. Statements like "the best tasting coffee" or "the fastest and most reliable" service provider cannot be confirmed objectively.

- **Unverified Claims**

  ◊ Many products promise to deliver results without providing any scientific evidence. Shampoo commercials that promise stronger, shinier hair do so without telling consumers why or how.

⬧ For example, yogurt maker Dannon paid $56 million USD in December 2010 to settle charges over claims that the probiotic bacteria in its yogurt could aid regularity and prevent colds or flu (CBC News, 2012).

- **Stereotyping Women**

    ⬧ Women in advertising have often been portrayed as sex objects or domestic servants. This type of advertising traffics in negative stereotypes and contributes to a sexist culture.

- **False Brand Comparisons**

    ⬧ Any time a company makes false or misleading claims about their competitors, they are spreading misinformation.

- **Children in Advertising**

    ⬧ Children consume huge amounts of advertising without being able to evaluate it objectively. Exploiting this innocence is one of the most common unethical marketing practices.

    ⬧ The maker of Nutella, the hazelnut, and chocolate spread, adored by children around the world, settled a class action lawsuit for $2.5 million USD in over its claims the treat was a healthy food. The lawsuit contended Nutella contained dangerous levels of saturated fat and was more than 55 percent processed sugar (CBC News, 2012).

- **Market Research**

    ⬧ Many research studies are just vehicles for pitching a sponsors product misuse of research findings.

- **Invasion of Privacy**

    ⬧ Companies are trusted with critical consumer information, which they must not take advantage of but use in an ethical manner.

- **Marketing Audience**

    ⬧ Selected marketing or unethical market exclusion of individuals within society because of race, gender, religion, and any other demographic variables.

- **Pricing Ethics**

    ⬧ Ethical pricing strategies are performed in order to earn profits without deceiving competitors or consumers.

The Canadian Marketing Association has crafted The CMA Code of Ethics and Standards of Practice. (A lengthy code of ethics and standards of practice for their members.) Though not law, their overarching ethical principles guide their membership, industry professionals, and government on what is acceptable and what the marketing industry should be communicating to consumers. They read as follows (Canadian Marketing Association, 2017):

1. Marketers *must promote responsible and transparent personal information management practices* in a manner consistent with the provisions of the *Personal Information Protection and Electronic Documents Act* (Canada).

2. Marketing communications *must not omit material facts and must be clear, comprehensible, and truthful.* Marketers must not knowingly make a representation to a consumer or business that is false or misleading.

3. Marketers *must not participate in any campaign involving the disparagement or exploitation of any person or group on the grounds of race, colour, ethnicity, religion, national origin, gender, sexual orientation, marital status, or age.*

4. Marketers *must not participate in the dissemination of unsolicited material that is sexually explicit, vulgar, or indecent in nature,* except where required to do so by law.

5. Marketers *must not participate in the dissemination of any material that unduly, gratuitously and without merit exploits sex, horror, mutilation, torture, cruelty, violence, or hate,* except where required to do so by law.

6. Marketers *must not knowingly exploit the credulity, lack of knowledge, or inexperience of any consumer, taking particular care when dealing with vulnerable consumers . . . "vulnerable consumer" includes . . . children, teenagers, people with disabilities, the elderly, and those for whom English or French is not their first language.*

Practice...

1. According to the Canadian Marketing Association, _____ are responsible for the content and practices of their marketing communication.
    a. consumers
    b. competitors
    c. marketers
    d. government

2. Surrogate advertisers:
    a. would advertise in a magazine.
    b. find ways to disguise cigarette and alcohol products without referencing them directly.
    c. convey negative messages about women in ads.
    d. tell customers that taking diet pills will make you lose 30 lbs in a week.

3. The maker of Nutella was charged $2.5 million because:
    a. its pricing to consumers was unethical and over the top.
    b. it exploited the innocence of children by making false claims about the product.
    c. it excluded certain members of the community like women and ethnics.
    d. it made a false brand comparison with a major peanut butter manufacturer.

4. The CMA Code of Ethics and Standards of Practice:
    a. is a law in Canada that marketers have to comply to.
    b. is a guide on how marketing and business professionals should conduct themselves.
    c. is exclusive only to marketers in Canada.
    d. states that marketers need to be transparent only when they are reprimanded by the federal government.

5. Companies that use critical consumer information, without their consent are:
    a. puffing up their products.
    b. selecting a market audience solely for the use of promoting a product or service.
    c. potentially stereotyping their customers.
    d. invading their privacy.

 **Apply...**

1. Answer the following in groups. You've come up with a new candy product that is fashioned to look like a cigarette. You'd like to distribute this item in Mac's convenience stores. Can you foresee any issues with this? Will Mac's want to distribute them? Explain.

    _____

    _____

    _____

    _____

    _____

    _____

    _____

    _____

    _____

    _____

    _____

    _____

    _____

2. Answer the following in groups. Victoria Secrets has a subsidiary (Pink) which sells clothing, underwear, bras, etc. to Generation Y. They have been looked upon as unfavourable in the fashion industry due to Generation Z buying this product. Click (https://tinyurl.com/flextext-vic-secrets) to learn more. Has Victoria secrets done anything wrong? Why or why not?

    _____

    _____

    _____

    _____

    _____

    _____

    _____

    _____

    _____

    _____

    _____

    _____

KNOW...

Learning Objectives

1. Ethics refers to the moral principles or values that generally govern the conduct of an individual or a group. Business ethics determine companies' everyday conduct. Laws define the boundaries of what is legal and are usually easier to determine. Mores are the rules people develop as a result of cultural norms and values. Ethics can be taught in business by providing training to employees to develop a personal set of ethical conduct. There are three levels of ethical development. They are pre-conventional, conventional, and post-conventional morality. The ways companies can manage ethics in their employees is to offer train and provide them with guidelines on what is acceptable.

2. Ethical marketing is less of a marketing strategy and more of a philosophy that informs all marketing efforts. It seeks to promote honesty, fairness, and responsibility in all advertising. Ethics is a notoriously difficult subject because everyone has subjective judgments about what is "right" and what is "wrong." For this reason, ethical marketing is not a hard and fast list of rules, but a general set of guidelines to assist companies as they evaluate new marketing strategies. If a product lives up to the claims made in its advertising, it reflects positively on the entire company and being ethical in your marketing efforts promotes the company, improves a company's image, and develops trust and long-term relationships with customers.

3. The CMA has come up with a list of what is acceptable and ethical when it comes to marketing. Though not a law, the principles act as an instruction to marketers, business, and government on what is acceptable and unethical. Unethical business practices include Surrogate Advertising, Exaggeration, Puffery, Unverified Claims, Stereotyping Women, False Brand Comparisons, Children in Advertising, Market Research, Invasion of Privacy, Marketing Audience, and Pricing Ethics.

Key Terms

Children in Advertising: Exploiting children to promote a product.

Ethical Marketing: Marketing which uses and incorporates social and environmental considerations in the development of products and the way they are promoted.

Ethics: Ethics are defined as . . . "the moral principles (or values) that govern a person's behaviour and identify what is good from what is bad".

Exaggeration: Advertisers using false claims about a product's quality or popularity. A slogan like "get coverage everywhere on earth" advertises features that cannot be delivered.

False Brand Comparisons: Any time a company makes false or misleading claims about their competitors.

Invasion of Privacy: Taking advantage of and misusing customer information.

Laws: The boundaries of what is legal and are the written guidelines that must be followed in society.

Marketing Audience: Selected marketing or unethical market exclusion of individuals within society because of race, gender, religion, and any other demographic variables.

Market Research: Misusing research findings to pitch a product.

Mores: The rules or parameters that people develop as a result of cultural norms and values. Mores are traditionally learned from childhood, culture, education, religion, etc. and are differentiated as either good or bad behaviour.

Pricing Ethics: Using unethical pricing strategies to market a product.

Puffery: When an advertiser relies on subjective rather than objective claims, they are puffing up their products. Statements like "the best tasting coffee" or "the fastest and most reliable" service provider cannot be confirmed objectively.

Stereotyping Women: Women in advertising have often been portrayed as sex objects or domestic servants. This type of advertising traffics in negative stereotypes and contributes to a sexist culture.

Surrogate Advertising: A method used by marketers to disguise products that are illegal to market like cigarettes and alcohol and not refer them directly.

Unverified Claims: Promising to deliver results without providing any scientific evidence. Shampoo commercials that promise stronger, shinier hair do so without telling consumers why or how.

Answers to Practice

Ethics and Business
1. b   2. b   3. b   4. a   5. d

Ethics and Marketing
1. b   2. a   3. b   4. a   5. d

Types of Unethical Marketing and Policies to Protect Unethical Marketing
1. c   2. b   3. b   4. b   5. d

References

American Marketing Association https://www.ama.org/resources/Pages/Dictionary.aspx?

Bhardwaj. (June, 2017). Ethical issues in marketing practices in India. *International Journal of Research in IT and Management (IJRIM), 7(6)*, 7–12.

"Brands up their game in ethical advertising", Marcie, MacLellan, The Guardian, December 10, 2015, https://www.theguardian.com/media-network/2015/dec/10/unethical-advertising-outdated-trend-feelgood-marketing.

Canadian Marketing Association, CMA's Code of Ethics and Standards of Practice, 2017,Reprinted with permission https://www.the-cma.org/regulatory/code-of-ethics.

Ethical Marketing. Retrieved from http://www.marketing-schools.org/types-of-marketing/ethical-marketing.html.

Financial Times, 2017, http://lexicon.ft.com/Term?term=ethical-marketing.

2011 National Business Ethics Survey: Workplace Ethics in Transition. *Ethics Resource Center,* January 1, 2012. p 18.

The Deloitte Millennial Survey. (2017). Retrieved from https://www2.deloitte.com/global/en/pages/about-deloitte/articles/millennialsurvey.html. p. 8.

Tanzeel Akhtar, How ethical innovations boost brand perceptions, Marketing Week, July 2, 2015, https://www.marketingweek.com/2015/07/02/how-ethical-innovations-boost-brand-perceptions/

13 Marketing Plan

LEARNING OBJECTIVES

L01 Understand the marketing planning process and its relation to the organization

L02 Define what a marketing plan is

L03 Understand why a marketing plan is needed and necessary

L04 Know the components and sections of the marketing plan

LEARN...

According to a report released by Marketo in 2014, 34% of marketing professionals who responded to their annual survey on planning, stated that they did not have a documented marketing plan for their business. The report also found that a documented marketing plan corresponded directly to overall satisfaction with the marketing team. Meaning that over 77% of respondents who had documented marketing plans, were extremely satisfied with their marketing teams, compared to only 12.5% of those who were extremely unsatisfied (Marketo, 2014).

Hard to believe that many "marketing professionals" are planning blindly. On the flipside, those who are planning are achieving significant progress, success, and satisfaction at work.

How were the marketing professionals who weren't planning setting goals and executing against them? What was their marketing plan? What were their goals and strategies for success? How were they measuring what they promised to do? How were they presenting and sharing their progress to management and clients?

The marketing plan is a comprehensive document or "blueprint" that guides and describes what activities the marketing team will need to take on in order to help the organization achieve objectives like increased awareness of a brand, increased market share, and/or increased profits. Building the marketing plan involves intrinsic knowledge of the plan's components, their purpose and function, and how they relate back to the organization's goals. It also outlines timelines, budgets, and team roles and responsibilities on who will effectively craft, communicate, execute, and measure the plan to reach desired outcomes.

This chapter will reinforce the value of a marketing plan and offer insight into the plan's various components, including specific strategies that a plan should have in order to help the organization achieve its goals.

What Is a Marketing Plan?

 Understand the marketing planning process and its relation to the organization

LO2 Define what a marketing plan is

Marketing planning involves deciding on various marketing strategies that will support the organization (and its brands, products, and services) to attain its overall business and strategic objectives. Marketing planning is consumer focused and aims to provide value and relationships with customers. It is intended to provide shorter term, and specific operational objectives, strategies, and direction on how the organization should achieve the targeted goals. The following diagram (Figure 1) explains the marketing planning process.

The **marketing plan** is the outcome of this structured planning process. It is the document written for the purpose of describing the current market position of a business and the marketing strategy, it will need to take in order to achieve its objectives.

The marketing plan is one of several official planning documents that are created at the business unit level in support of (Figure 2):

- the **corporate business plan**
  ◇ commences at corporate level
  ◇ outlines a company's overall financial and operational objectives and strategies
  ◇ provides the corporate vision and philosophy

- the **corporate strategic plan**
  ◇ commences at corporate level
  ◇ describes the general long-term strategic direction that each business unit (like marketing) will take onto achieve the businesses' objectives and mission

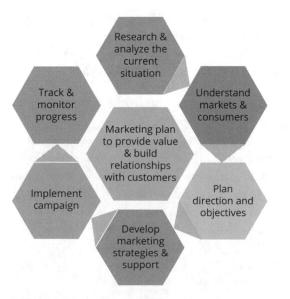

FIGURE 1 Marketing planning process.

Source: Based on Wood. *The Marketing Plan Handbook*, Pearson: Prentice Hall; 2008. p. 4.

Corporate
Business
Planning

Corporate
Strategic
Planning

Business Unit
Marketing
Planning

FIGURE 2 Marketing planning and its relation to the corporate business plan. Marketing planning is one of the many business units that will decide on strategies that will support a company's overall strategic objectives.

A marketing plan is defined as,

> . . . a document covering a particular period that summarizes what the marketer has learned about the marketplace, what will be accomplished through marketing, and how. All marketing plans should explain intended strategies for building relationships by creating, communicating, and delivering value to customers; outline the activities that employees will undertake to reach objectives, including gaining value for the organization; show the mechanisms for measuring progress towards objectives; and allow for adjustments if actual results are off course or the environment shifts. (Based on http://www.marketingprofs.com/3/mazzara1.asp)

It is important to note that the marketing plan is not a fixed document or one that is etched in stone. It is a living, breathing document that can be impacted by internal and external environmental variables such as shifts in corporate philosophy, market conditions, demand and supply, pricing issues, and new technology. Therefore, marketing planning is an ongoing process and the marketer is allowed to change the marketing plan in order for the company to achieve its objectives and keep up with changes that may occur in the market.

Also, the marketing plan cannot be implemented without the approval of key stakeholders within the organization such as management, operations, product development, finance, sales, HR, and of course, marketing.

Practice...

1. The Strategic Marketing Planning process consists of a series of logical steps and these steps can be aggregated into four phases. Which of the following is *not* included in the phases of the strategic marketing planning?
   a. Defining marketing strategy
   b. Setting the right mission and corporate goals
   c. Reviewing the current situation
   d. Formulating strategy

2. The _____ process commences at corporate level. Here the organization sets out it will support the company's overall mission, purpose, and values.
   a. researching
   b. strategic planning
   c. controlling
   d. managing

3. Which of the following is not a business unit that supports the organization?
   a. The marketing department
   b. The finance department
   c. The labour union that supports employee grievances
   d. The HR department

4. A marketing plan is a _____ document that can change at any time.
   a. variable
   b. fixed
   c. corporate
   d. operations

5. Marketing planning aims to provide:
   a. value and relationships with customers.
   b. value and relationships with internal corporate stakeholders.
   c. value and relationships with the strategic planning team.
   d. value and relationships with product suppliers and distributors.

 **Apply...**

1. Individually, answer the following. A friend of yours is considering to open a business but not complete a marketing plan prior to opening their store front. Give this entrepreneur several reasons why he/she should consider writing a marketing plan right away. Explain why marketing plans are so important to an organization.

_____

_____

_____

_____

_____

_____

_____

_____

_____

_____

_____

_____

_____

_____

_____

2. Individually, answer the following. Why does a marketing plan need to be flexible? Give examples of internal and/or external factors which could influence the plan and require it to be modified.

_____

_____

_____

_____

_____

_____

_____

_____

_____

_____

_____

_____

_____

_____

_____

What Is the Purpose of a Marketing Plan?

LO3 Understand why a marketing plan is needed and necessary

A good marketing plan will help the marketing team to answer key questions about their business and act as a reference document that will help them to execute the marketing strategy. It will also help to develop a structured approach to create services and products that satisfy your customers' needs.

For example, a marketing plan might have an objective to increase the organization's market share by 10%. The plan would then outline the strategies to support the objective and then the various tactics that need to be implemented in order to reach a 10% increase in market share.

The following are some reasons in support of the marketing plan.

- Answers key questions about your business
  - ◊ A marketing plan helps the marketer understand the company, its brand, products, and services, as well as support the company's mission and its overarching plans.

- Helps with "Big Picture" focus
  - ◊ The plan helps the marketing team to understand what the corporate goals are and to become customer-focused. It also empowers them to make decisions that are consistent with the company's objectives.

- Serves as a handbook and calendar
  - ◊ The marketing plan assigns specific tasks for the year and helps to keep you on track.

- Documents and records the plan of attack
  - ◊ The written document lays out the marketer's game plan. If people leave, if new people arrive, if memories falter, the information in the written marketing plan stays intact.

- Serves as a business reference
  - ◊ The marketing plan helps the marketer to assess the company's strengths, weaknesses, opportunities, and threats.

- Provides a "look in the mirror"
  - ◊ Shows a company its strengths, weaknesses, and any opportunities and threats (SWOT) that may be in your market or approaching

- Gives clarity to who your market and target audience is
  - ◊ The marketing plan allows you to find the clients and customers that are a "best fit" for your brand

- Helps you to craft marketing messages that are customer and results focussed
  - ◊ By knowing the nuances and needs of your target audience, the marketing plan will the marketer come up with the best course of action and most appropriate media and messages for the target.

- Charts success
  - ◊ The marketing plan helps the marketing team to chart the plan's final destination point. It's almost like a personal GPS that provides focus and attention and navigation them through competitive territory.

- Tracks success
  ◊ The marketing plan becomes a living document for measuring sales success, customer retention, product development, and sales initiatives.

- Tracks costs/Measures value
  ◊ A marketing plan provides a step-by-step guide to what and when the marketer is spending money on. It enables them to budget marketing expenses, as well as the success of your marketing efforts.

- Is a document to build on for the future
  ◊ Once the plan is complete, it will serve as a template for future marketing plans. The marketer can reapply successes and tweak any inconsistencies or weaker strategies and tactics (Mazzara, 2003).

 **Practice...**

1. The marketing plan will:
   a. assess the need for more corporate employees.
   b. address the necessary steps and actions that need to be taken in order to achieve the plan's objectives.
   c. demonstrate if the organization's mission is aligned with the corporation's goals.
   d. validate the need for a new corporate board of directors.

2. Which of the following is not a purpose of the marketing plan?
   a. To clearly show the plan's objectives and strategies
   b. Develop a structured approach to create services and products that satisfy your customers' needs
   c. Create a strategy for increased personnel and human resources
   d. A reference document that informs the team of the marketing strategy

3. The company's new president would like to know the cost and social media tactics used by the company this year. The best document to resort to would be:
   a. the company's strategic plan.
   b. the accounting department's budget reports.
   c. the company's mission statement.
   d. the company's marketing plan.

4. SWOT is an acronym for:
   a. strategy, working, opinion, tactical.
   b. strategy, weakness, opinions, tactics.
   c. strengths, weaknesses, opportunities, threats
   d. strategy, work, openness, toughness.

5. Which of the following is *not* a rationale or purpose for a marketing plan?
   a. Marketing plan assigns specific tasks for the year.
   b. It presents the media and messaging tactics that will most suit the target audience.
   c. It shows the marketing team and the organization how costly a campaign can be.
   d. It helps to motivate employees.

 **Apply...**

1. One section of the marketing plan involves the marketer completing a SWOT analysis. Assume Nike wishes to create a product line (shoes, clothing, etc.) for Spartan Racing (https://www.spartan.com/en). Reebok currently is the main sponsor for this sport. What would your SWOT look like?

_____

_____

_____

_____

_____

_____

_____

_____

_____

_____

_____

_____

_____

2. Continuing with Nike and Spartan racing, develop a profile for what a Spartan racer would look like. Not sure how to create the profile? Click on this link to learn how to develop a profile: https://tinyurl.com/flextext-target.

_____

_____

_____

_____

_____

_____

_____

_____

_____

_____

_____

_____

Marketing Plan Outline

LO4 Know the components and sections of the marketing plan

Though the exact contents, length, and format of a marketing plan may vary, the template for most marketing plans is consistent. Sections are generally drafted in the order they appear in the plan, with each successive section building on the previous one. For example, marketing managers will not be able to select a target audience strategy for a new product until a situation analysis has been conducted analyzing the market and the company's position in it. Similarly, budgets and costs to execute a marketing campaign cannot be prepared unless objectives, strategies, and action programs have been set.

The following outlines the major sections of the marketing plan and its purpose:

Executive Summary

Though first on the list, the Executive Summary is completed last. This section of the plan highlights the objectives and summarizes each of the other sections of the marketing plan. The executive summary is helpful in giving the marketer and other higher members of the organization an overview of the plan's major points and how it links to the organizational goals and strategies.

Current Marketing Situation

This *marketing situation or situation analysis* section of the plan, allows the marketer to research, collect, and organize data about the market the organization is currently in, as well as the competitive dynamics it faces. It also looks at patterns, customers, and the current sales volume for the industry as a whole. The section summarizes environmental trends including:

- An internal and external situation analysis (that is, the company's mission, offerings, markets, previous results, and distribution) and

- A SWOT (internal strengths and weaknesses and external opportunities and threats) analysis that will help management to anticipate important positive or negative developments that might have an impact on the firm and its strategies.

Objectives and Issues

After the marketing has a handle on the current situation, they need to think about what objectives are appropriate and realistic at this time. The objectives section addresses what the marketer specifically wants the marketing plan to accomplish and what key issues may affect their success. Marketing objectives are quantified, measurable goals, such as *"grow market share by 5% by the end of the year"* or *"shift 25% of our catalogue consumers over to website ordering"*. The most effective way to define your marketing objectives is to follow the "SMART" acronym:

- Specific: have clearly outlined quantitative objectives

- Measurable: indicate what you intend to use as a measure of success

- Achievable: make sure that the objectives that are set out, are attainable for the business

- Realistic: make sure that you have the knowledge of resources to achieve your objectives

- Timely: be clear about the time-frame in which you intend to achieve your objectives

Marketing Strategy

Develop the marketing and promotion strategies that the organization will use.

An effective marketing strategy will help to define the overall direction of the marketing program and what the marketer will do to support and achieve the marketing objectives.

The strategy section details the marketing and promotion strategies that the team is going to use to bring the marketer's products and services to market in ways that will satisfy and add value to their customers. Strategies to consider

The strategy section includes:

- A rationale for the selection of a target audience and a description of the customers you are targeting by defining their demographic and psychographic profile and their wants and needs as they relate to the products and/or services offered by the company.

- The positioning you desire in the market that will cause you to stand out from the competition and allow you to be a market leader

- A Unique Selling Proposition (USP)

- Specific strategies for each element of the marketing mix including advertising, direct marketing, training programs, trade shows, and e-commerce websites and social media.

Marketing Implementation

This is the section that turns the marketing plan into marketing actions to achieve the strategic marketing objectives. It spells out the specific programs or *tactics* that will be used to support marketing strategy. Some examples of tactics include newspaper advertising, trade shows, blogs, e-newsletters, and radio ads. Implementation will also answer the "nitty gritty" types of questions like: What will be done? When will it be done? Where will it be done? Who will do it? How much will it cost?

Budget

A budget or financial will detail the expected revenues and costs of production, distribution, and marketing. The budget is based on the marketing programs that are proposed in the marketing plan. The marketing manager needs to review what they hope to accomplish with the marketing plan, review their current financial situation, and then allocate funding for the marketing plan.

An Evaluation and Monitoring of the Marketing Plan

To ensure ongoing improvement, it's critical to test and measure your plan's progress, as well as the results of your marketing activities. Whatever method or technology you choose to use, formal methods of evaluation and monitoring will help you to:

- understand the effectiveness of your marketing
- identify the strategies that are and are not working
- gauge the return on investment
- review products and campaigns that are not meeting their goals
- assign contingency plans if necessary

Practice...

1. What would the main objective for the "competition" part of any marketing plan be?
   a. It should describe how well its competitors are doing in the market.
   b. The plan should describe the company's competition and how the organization will be different from its competitor.
   c. It should budget direct marketing.
   d. It should describe how the organization would destroy its competition.

2. Which of the following would be an example of a marketing goal?
   a. Increase staff by 100 employees by the end of 2020.
   b. Decrease the overall cost of production by 10%.
   c. Authorized dividends for stockholders.
   d. Increase sales of our men's deodorant line by 10% in 1 year.

3. An ice cream factory has completed its marketing research and found that the south west region of Canada has a higher demand for mint chocolate chip ice cream than any other region. How might the marketing budget reflect this consumer need?
   a. Increase in social media marketing
   b. Increase in operations for the region
   c. Increase in overall marketing
   d. Increase in geographically defined advertising

4. Which of the following is the first step of the marketing plan outline?
   a. Create the market plan budget
   b. Monitor the marketing plan results
   c. Develop the marketing plan goals
   d. Do market research and collect data on the internal and external environment the marketer will face

5. How long is usually the lifespan of marketing plans?
   a. 10–15 years
   b. 20–25 years
   c. 6–10 years
   d. 1–5 years

Apply...

1. Continuing with Nike and Spartan racing, develop a product that you believe Nike should be selling to the profile group you targeted. What would that product be? How much would it cost? How would you promote the product?

_____

_____

_____

_____

_____

_____

_____

_____

_____

_____

_____

_____

2. Continuing with Nike and Spartan racing, explain what your USP will be. Click on this link to learn more about USP: https://tinyurl.com/flextext-usp

_____

_____

_____

_____

_____

_____

_____

_____

_____

_____

_____

_____

KNOW...

Learning Objectives

1. One of the most important documents of any business unit is the plan developed by the marketing team. A marketing plan is a business document that is written for the purpose of describing the current market position of a business and its marketing strategy. It is a roadmap that provides the marketer and the organization with information and the direction that is required towards reaching the high-level objectives set by the organization. The marketing plan supports the overall business plan and corporate strategy and needs to be referred to and assessed frequently because of always changing internal and external environmental factors. Because of these changes, the plan is not fixed and can be changed by the marketer at any time in order to be in tune with environmental changes.

2. The purpose of a marketing plan is to clearly show what steps or actions will be taken to achieve the marketing plan's goals. For example, a marketing plan might have a strategy to increase the organization's market share by 10%. The plan would then outline the goals that need to be achieved in order to reach a 10% increase in market share. Some of the reasons for a plan include: Answers key questions about your business; Helps with "Big Picture" focus; Serves as a handbook and calendar; Documents and records the plan of attack; Serves as a business reference; Provides clarity on who your market and target audience is; Helps you craft marketing messages that will generate results; Charts success; Tracks success; Tracks costs/ Measures value; and Is a document to build on for the future.

3. Marketing plans usually cover a period of 1–5 years. The plan is developed by looking at the current market, setting strategies, creating a budget, making goals, and, finally, following-up. The plan is a detailed map of what the organization hopes to accomplish over a given period of time and incorporates the following sections: An executive summary a current marketing situation, objectives and issues, marketing strategy, marketing implementation, budget, implementation controls, and an evaluation and monitoring section.

Key Terms

Corporate Business Plan: Outlines a company's overall financial and operational objectives and strategies.

Corporate Strategic Plan: Describes the general long-term strategic direction that each business unit of the company (like marketing) will take on to achieve the businesses' objectives and mission.

Marketing Plan: A business document written for the purpose of describing the current market position of a business and its marketing strategy for the period covered by the marketing plan.

Marketing Planning: Involves deciding on various marketing strategies that will help the company to attain its overall strategic objectives.

Answers to Practice

What Is a Marketing Plan?
1. b   2. b   3. c   4. a   5. a

What Is the Purpose of a Marketing Plan?
1. b   2. c   3. d   4. c   5. d

Marketing Plan Outline
1. b   2. d   3. d   4. d   5. d

References

Marketo. *Marketing Trend Watch,* 2014 Planning Edition. 2014. pp. 3–4.

Mazzara G. (March 18, 2003). Why do we need a marketing plan anyway? *Marketing Profs*. Retrieved from http://www.marketingprofs.com/3/mazzara1.asp.

Wood. *The Marketing Plan Handbook,* Pearson: Prentice Hall; 2008. p. 4.

Notes

Notes